Pakistan-Afghanistan Relations: Pashtunistan Factor

Pakistan-Afghanistan Relations:
Pashtunistan Factor

Dr Muzammil Ahad
and
Professor P. Moorthy

KALPAZ

First Published, 2017

Published by

Kalpaz Publications
C-30, Satyawati Nagar,
Delhi – 110052
E-mail: kalpaz@hotmail.com
Ph.: 9212142040

Printed at: G. Print Process, Delhi

Cataloging in Publication Data—DK
Courtesy: D.K. Agencies (P) Ltd. <docinfo@dkagencies.com>

Ahad, Muzammil, author.
Pakistan-Afghanistan relations : Pashtunistan factor / Dr. Muzammil Ahad & Professor P. Moorthy.
pages cm
ISBN 9789351282792

1. Pakistan—Foreign relations—Afghanistan. 2. Afghanistan—Foreign relations—Pakistan. 3. Pushtuns—Pakistan. 4. Pushtuns—Afghanistan. I. Moorthy, P. (Periakrishna), 1956- author. II. Title.

DS383.5.A3A33 2017 DDC 327.54910581 23

CONTENTS

FOREWORD

The book "Pakistan-Afghanistan Relations: Pashtunistan Factor" authored by Dr Muzammil Ahad, and Professor P. Moorthy attempts to historicise the Pashtunistan issue and presents it in Pakistani, Afghanistani and Pashtuni perspectives. It also makes an effort to study the colonial legacy of the Durand Line, which serves as a border between Afghanistan and Pakistan, as a successor state to British India.

The Durand Line proved to be a bone of contention between the two countries. Afghanistan holds the view that the agreement of the Durand Line was signed by it under duress and demands that the right to self-determination for the Pakhtoons living on Pakistan side, who, it pleads, were forcibly separated from their motherland. Afghanistan also asserts that it is the legitimate protector of Pakhtoons living on the other side of the border. On the other hand, Pakistan, being a successor state of the British India, holds that it had inherited the Durand boundary as an international frontier and that Pakhtoons on its side had already expressed their support to Pakistan in the referendum held in 1947. For Pakistan, therefore, the question of self-determination does not arise and it categorically refuses to negotiate with Afghanistan on Pashtunistan issue. Thus, the Pashtunistan Factor has assumed a great significance in the Afghanistan-Pakistan relations.

This book is a welcome addition to the knowledge on the subject and be of great use to the scholars and students who are interested in this issue.

Dr B. Krishnamurthy
Professor and Head
Department of Politics and
International Studies,
Pondicherry University
(A Central University)

Preface

Located at the cross-roads of Central, South and West Asia and sharing borders with Central Asia, on the north, Chinese province of Xinjiang in the east, Iran on the west and south-west, and Pakistan and Pakistan Administered Kashmir on the south and south-east, Afghanistan occupies a unique geo-strategic position in the region. During the past quarter century, Afghanistan has remained turbulent posing great challenges to peace and security in and around the region.

Afghanistan and Pakistan both SAARC members enjoy a long common border of 2500 km known as Durand Line. Despite share geography, ethnicity and faith, relations between both neighbours have never been smooth. Rather, they have been problematic.

In this book an attempt has been made to analyse Afghanistan-Pakistan relations which have not been cordial in spite of geographical contiguity and identity of religion, culture and economic interests of the two countries. Though immediately after independence, Pakistan made overtures to the Muslim countries in an attempt to seek Islamic leadership, its efforts proved fruitless and its relations with Afghanistan remained far from normal.

The study of Afghan-Pak relations demonstrates and manifests the attitude and behaviour of Pakistan elite towards a fellow Muslim country when there is a clash of interests. It is the Common historical background a legacy of the colonial rule in Asia that provides a basis for understanding the strained relations between these two Muslim countries. In fact, tensions and hostilities among many countries of the third world are a legacy of imperialism and colonialism.

The Durand Line delineated in 1893 by the British between the British India and Afghanistan, subsequently inherited by Pakistan as a successor state to British India, proved to be a bone of contention between the two countries. Afghanistan's main argument is that the agreement of the Durand Line was signed by it under duress.

It demanded the right to self-determination for the Pakhtoons living on Pakistan side, which, it's pleaded, were forcibly separated from their motherland. Afghanistan asserts that it is the legitimate protector of Pakhtoons living on the other side of the border. On the other hand Pakistan, being a successor state to the British India, holds that it had inherited the Durand boundary as an international frontier and that Pakhtoons on its side had already expressed their support in referendum held in 1947. For Pakistan, therefore, the question of self-determination does not arise. It refused to negotiate with Afghanistan on Pakhtoonistan issue. But Afghanistan attached great importance to the issue and its rulers wanted to solve the problem before improving their relations with Pakistan.

This book specifically deals with the issue of Pakhtoonistan and the Durand Line that has been challenging the intensification of relation between two neighbouring states of Afghanistan and Pakistan which has not only been major source of instability but also barrier before cementing of trade, political, cultural and economic ties between two states and as hurdle before regional cooperation in the SAARC region.

ACKNOWLEDGEMENT

This work was supported by Department of Politics and International Studies, Pondicherry University. We sincerely thank our colleagues from the said Department who provided insight and expertise that greatly assisted the research, although they may not agree with all of the interpretations and conclusions of this book.

The association with scholars like Professor Dr N.K. Jha, Dr M. Pillai, Dr L. Samraj, and Dr Raju at DPIS Professor Nalini Kant Jha (DPIS), Professer Mohanan B. Pillai (DPIS), Professor Lazarus Samraj (DPIS), Professor A. Subramanyam Raju (UMISARC), Professor G. Chandrika (History), Professor Venkata Rangnotam (History) Pondicherry University has helped in improving the manuscript. We would like to show our sincere gratitude to all these eminent scholars and professors.

Chapter-I

Introduction

Afghanistan shares long border of 2500 Km with the neighbouring Pakistan. The long border not only retains significant role in evaluation of historical relations between two countries but this assessment maintains vital role in strained relations since the formation of Pakistan. Doubtlessly Pakistan carried huge role in the transformation of Afghanistan in last half century.

Pakistan and its relations with Afghanistan plays major role in instability of Afghanistan. It has also laid harmful consequence on various aspects including political, social, economy, military and religious dimensions. How the relations between Afghanistan and Pakistan created and developed? What is the dilemma between Afghanistan and Pakistan? How developed countries played their role in relations between these two countries? What Afghanistan and Pakistan expect from each other? Is there any solution to the Afghanistan and Pakistan crisis?

Since 1947, relations between Pakistan and Afghanistan have remained strained. Sometimes they have even reached to the brink of war. The framework of Pakistan's foreign policy towards Afghanistan carries the deep imprint of the British imperialist heritage of treating that country as buffer and of defending the legality of the Durand Line as the international border.

Throughout the nineteenth century, Great Britain had to consider with the menace of the expansion of Tsarist Russia in Central Asia. It regarded the Russian penetration in the Central Asian region as a potential threat to its imperial interest in India.

The fear of Russia became the decisive factor in British frontier policy in India, and close relations with Afghanistan were considered essential to safeguard India from Russian expansionism. In Britain, two schools of thought emerged out of the Debate on How best to meet Russian threat. These were known as the Close Border Policy School and the Forward Policy School.

The Close Border Policy meant direct British rule in the settled areas of the frontier region and leaving the tribes to administer their own affairs. It also implied non-interference in Afghan affairs. British policy-makers believed that a friendly and stable Afghanistan would make an effective deterrent against Russian expansionism.

It was, therefore, necessary for the British to abstain from the military expeditions in Afghanistan and to keep out of the internecine conflicts of that country. During the 1980s this Close Border Policy of Stationary Policy was given up in favour of the Forward Policy. Under the new policy the British assumed the responsibility of administering certain tribal areas and moved strong garrisons forward into the other parts of the region.

They also force Afghanistan's Amir Abdur Rehman to accept a border settlement which pushed the border from the eastern foot hills to their crest.[1] Successive British military expeditions combined with the British Policy of Playing off one faction against another with ruling family led to almost total subjugation of Afghanistan during the latter half of nineteenth century.

This book attempts to explain the historical perspective of 'Pashtunistan' issue. The discussion has also been drawn to explain the contestation over Durand Line and objections raised by Afghan rulers. Similarly, the various perspectives of the governments in Afghanistan and Pakistan have been discussed. The views of Pashtu people also finds specific amount of discussion in this book. The book has been specifically elaborated upon the Afghan-Pak relations with reference to Pakhtoonistan issue. It has raised two serious issues between two neighbours; one is over the Durand Line and the second is Pashtun Identity inside Pakistan. Afghans argue that the Durand Line is the imperialistic outcome of British and USSR. Therefore the demarcation of border was relevant to British period only. They have questioned the relevance of Durand Line for present times and asked for the right of self-determination for Pashtuns.

Since the creation of Pakistan in 1947 Pakhtoonistan became the core of stressed and tense relations between Pakistan and Afghanistan. It has often led to border skirmishes, propaganda warfare, and closure of diplomatic ties and blockade of Afghan trade transit via Pakistan.[2]

The dispute between two nations first surfaced in the United Nations on September 30, 1947 when Afghanistan stands against Pakistan's admission into UN.[3] Hosyan Aziz the then representative of Afghanistan explained it to General Assembly:

> We cannot recognise the North West Frontier as part of Pakistan solutions as long as people of North West Frontier have not been given an opportunity free from any kind of influence and I repeat, free from any kind of interference to determine for themselves whether they wish to be independent or to become part of Pakistan.[4]

An impartial plebiscite was demanded by Afghanistan for Pakistan Pastun region. The territorial boundaries of Afghanistan were unacceptable for Afghanistan. Afghanistan government claimed that Pakistan had to re-demarcate the boundaries to get international community recognition as a complete state. Propaganda was often played by Afghanistan to instigate the Pashtu tribes to create an independent Afghanistan.

A friendship treaty was signed between Zaheer Shah and Pakistan in November 1947 which remained vague and ineffective. However, the diplomatic ties were resumed during 1948.[5] Some conciliatory efforts were made towards each other when Afghanistan withdrew its negative vote at UN and exchange of ambassadors took place. The goodwill gesture was initiated by Afghanistan after appointing the uncle of Zaheer Shah, H.H. Shah Wali Khan as Pakistan ambassador. Shah Wali presented his credentials to Pakistan on May 08, 1948 to Jinnah. Jinnah said on this occasion:

> Your royal highness has rightly referred to the natural bonds of friendship and affection which bind people of our two countries. It could hardly be otherwise as these bonds are based on ties of faith and culture. With such powerful bonds in our favour we cannot. I feel, fail to bring the people of our two countries closure than they were before the birth of Pakistan.[6]

Pashtunistan issue was on high alert immediately after 1947. King Zaheer Shah in his inaugural speech during *Shina-i-Milli* on May 26, 1948 referred to the Pakhoonistan issue:

> .... the Afghan nation welcomed and viewed with utmost gratification the establishment of the dominion of Pakistan and India and the Afghan government did not fail in exerting their best efforts to take up the matter of our Afghan brethren living in the government of Great Britain and the newly set up government did not fail in exerting their best efforts to take up the matter of our Afghan brethren living in the government of Great Britain and the newly set up government in Pakistan. Whilst we have openly declared our desire to set up an embassy of Afghanistan in Karachi, with a view to cementing the relationship and 'Bon Voisinage' with

> Pakistan, we earnestly hope that assurances in this regard will be dully implemented.[7]

Loya Jirga the Afghan National Assembly has rejected all treaties and agreements between Pakistan and Afghanistan entered into before 1948. They declared that they don't recognise the Durand Line and also declared the agreements null and void. Loya Jirga has also announced the separation of North Western Frontier Provinces from Pakistan and ensured all possible help for the same for the people of this region.[8]

Afghanistan mobilised the troops to Pakistan side in March 1949, however, Pakistan closed the border for three months and the Afghan activities were failed. The situation was aggravated when the Pashtu people first opened their Provincial Parliament in 1950. Mirza Ali Khan of Afridi clan became its first president. They held the meetings at different places with tacit support of Afghanistan and all the clans had ensured their support for it.

Pakistan in response to this on January 1950 asked British government to declare the Durand Line as International Border and attempts to encroach upon it as violation of common wealth border. Philip Noel, Secretary of State for Common Wealth Relations while speaking in a conference on January 12, 1950 said;

> "...under International Law Pakistan was the lawful inheritor of the rights and duties of the Indian Government of the regions on the Pakistan side of Durand Line."[9]

Later in 1950 British Parliament confirmed the Durand Line and declared it an International Border.[10]

The Pashtu tribal people started an uprising for autonomy demand for Pashtu territory. The Pakistani government in turn used brute forces to curb the uprising and quell out the demand for autonomy. During the period of March to October 1950 Pakistan government used heavy bombardment on Pashtu villages killing innocent men, women and children. One of the aeroplanes bombed a village across the frontier in Afghanistan. Pakistan accepted the responsibility of the accidental bombing and offered the full payment; however, it could not help the settlement of issue. Afghanistan continuously used it as the propaganda against Pakistan.

In Delhi, a journal with the name Pashtunistan was published in 1951 and circulated internationally. The Pashtunistan day was celebrated in Kabul, Delhi and London with mixed political rituals and funfair. In Kabul, a road square was renamed as Pashtunistan Square. The map showing the Pashtunistan including NWFP, Chitral and Pashtu areas of Baluchistan extending from the Durand Line to Indus was published in a journal, *Arif*.[11]

Another nuisance in their relations was the assassination of Prime Minister Liaqat Ali Khan in 1951 by Syed Akbar an exiled Afghan citizen in Pakistan. However, Pakistan accepted the Afghan government's refusal of any involvement in the killing.

The large scale protests were erupted in Kabul and other parts of Afghanistan on March 27, 1950 against Pakistan policy to make Pakistan one unit. They perceived it as disastrous for the very concept of Pashtunistan and its autonomy. In retaliation protests were held in Pakistan against Kabul. Therefore, consequentially fighting started on border. Pakistan argued it was started by Afghanistan; however, Afghan government took it as a fight between Pashtu's and Pakistan military.[12]

Pakistan closed the Afghan consulates in Pakistan on May 2, 1955. Trade agencies were also banished in Peshawar, Quetta and Chaman. It was the mark of protest against Afghan government. They also warned Afghan government of closure of border and economic sanctions. The Afghan government mobilised the troops on the Pakistani side borders which aroused counter-response from Pakistan.

The tension was released after the mediation from Egypt, Saudi Arabia, Iran and Turkey.[13]

The relations were resumed normal in February 1958 when Zahir Shah visited Pakistan and an agreement was signed in May 1958 for improving transit facilities for Afghanistan via Pakistan. Afghanistan refused to renew and issue visas to Pakistan officials working in American and British embassies in Afghanistan in July 1960 in the backdrop of deteriorated situations.

Pakistan in 1955 conceived concept of one unit for which the ruler of Dir refused to surrender and Afghanistan mobilised its troops towards the border for his support. Pakistan in retaliation also concentrated its military to Dir border and situation escalated into clashes lasting for 1961 to 1963 period. A blame game of incursion and intrusion started between two nations. Pakistan blamed Afghanistan for sending its militia in facade of tribes' men inside Pakistan. Afghanistan, however, denied such claims and put blame on Pakistan creating trouble in Afghan territory. Afghans further blamed Pakistan for undemocratic and repressive behaviour meted out to Pashtu. Pakistani media has always claimed it as a baseless propaganda.[14]

The fighting took place in Bajaur area between Pakistan and Afghanistan in August 1961. Pakistan closed its consulates in Afghanistan and asked the Afghanistan to follow the suit. Afghanistan quite contrary presented its conditions before Pakistan for meaningful future diplomatic relations: Pakistan should guarantee the right to Self determination of Pashtu tribes, its troops should withdraw from tribal areas of Durand Line, it has to release detained Pashtu leaders and Afghan consulates and trade agencies should be reopened in Pakistan.[15]

Pakistan denied accepting any of the above conditions and Afghanistan severed the relations with Pakistan and closed border.[16] Pakistan as usual put restrictions on seasonal movement of Afghan nomads into Pakistan.

The traffic was also stopped and the crops which were ready to export to India were airlifted by USSR to India.

These kinds of Provocations by Afghanistan over Pashtunistan lead Pakistan to impose trade embargo on Afghanistan three times, 1950, 1955 and 1961-63.[17] However, embargo was lifted on mediation of Shah of Iran. The issue of Pashtunistan and Durand Line was again renewed to build a pressure on Pakistan not to take advantages of Sino-Indian war of 1961-62.[18] A Pakistan-Afghan-Iran convention was prescribed by Ayub Khan which was not given due concern by Afghanistan.

However, Tehran Accord was signed in May 28, 1963 on the mediation of Shah of Iran. A joint communiqué regarding the Accord was issued from Tehran, Rawalpindi and Kabul simultaneously on May 30, 1963, the features of the Communique include the opening of consulates, re-establishing trade agencies, regularising trade and transit arrangements, following international law and treaties, create atmosphere of goodwill and friendship, re-open consulates at Pashawar, Quetta, Khandhar and Jalalabad.[19]

The borders were re-opened in 1963 and the economic issues of Afghanistan were solved. Around two Lakh Afghan Powindahs was restored by 1963. The Dir issue was resolved by integrating it into West Pakistan. Zulfikar Ali was Foreign Minister who declared Pashtunistan a "completely closed and a dead issue."[20]

Afghan government announced in 1963 that Pashtu issue is the only difference and would be resolved peacefully. A five-year transit agreement was signed during March 1965. Afghanistan, despite its differences, was sympathetic to Pakistan during 1965 war and resisted Russian pressure to exploit Pashtu issue against Pakistan. Later in 1966 and 1967 the heads of two states visited each other's countries.[21]

During the period of 1969 to 1971 Af-Pak relations were normal and the avenues were found to open up economic trade and import export opportunities. Pakistan offered technical assistance in the form of medicine, engineering and irrigation.[22] The relations during the Zaheer Shah period were cordial towards Pakistan, however, differences are persistently between two nations on Pashtu question. He followed moderate views on the international issues and for the Dir and border clashes between Af-Pak he said that:

> "We are partly to blame for the incident, but the Pakistanis were not without guilt and that Pakistan with rapidly expanding army equipped with American arms, posed a threat to Afghanistan."[23]

Afghanistan again during 1971 war with India remained sympathetic for territorial integrity of Pakistan and expressed its goodwill and non-interference in the war.[24] Though, the squabble over Pashtunistan was persistently hurting the cordial relations between two neighbouring nations. However, they have entered into several mutual agreements and treaties to facilitate trade and transit avenues for each other. During Prime Minister Bhutto's visit to Afghanistan in 1972 he praised Afghanistan for their restraint during 1965 and 1971 war. He also ensured commitment of establishing cordial relations between two nations. By the year 1975 Afghanistan subsided the Pashtunistan issue and stopped symbolising Pashtunistan Day. The hostilities have passed but the relations could not last long peacefully.

References

1. James, W Spaiin, "Political Problems of Borderland," in Ainslie T. Embree, ed., Pakistan's Western Borderlands (New Delhi, 1977), p. 11.
2. Hyman, A, *Afghanistan Under Soviet domination: 1964-81*, The Macmillan Press Ltd., London, UK, 1982, p. 46.
3. 82 Sally Ann Bynard, "Historical Setting", in Nyrop and Seekins, eds. *Afghanistan: A country Study*, (Foreign Area Studies: The American University, 1986), p. 55.
4. Mohammad Ahsen Chaudhry, *Pakistan and World Security*, (Karachi: Royal Book Company, 1987), p. 101.

Azmat Hayat Khan, *The Durand Line: it's Geostrategic*, (University of Peshawar: Area Study Centre, 2000), p. 187.

5. Zarina Salamat, *Pakistan 1947-58: A Historical Review*, (Islamabad: National Institute of Historical and Cultural Research, 1992), p. 191.
6. Government of Pakistan, "Presentation of Credentials to the Quaid-e-Azam by Sardar Najibullah Khan," Special Representative of his Majesty, the Afghan King, F.125 (11)-GG/47.
7. Fazal-ur-Rahim Marwat, *The Evolution and Growth of Communism in Afghanistan 1917-79: An Appraisal*, (Karachi: Royal Book Company, 1997), pp. 277-278.
8. Salamat, Pakistan: 1947-58, p. 191.
9. *Ibid.*, p. 192.
10. Abdul Manan Bazai, "An Assessment of Pak-Afghan Relations: Since 1947 to 2001," Ph.D. thesis, University of Balochistan, Pakistan Research Repository, 2008, p. 26.
11. Fazal Haque Kazi, *Law and Politics in Pakistan*, (Karachi: Royal Book Company, 1976), p. 194.
12. Kulwant Kaur, "Pak-Afghan Relations," in Surrendra Chopra, ed. *Perspective on Pakistan's Foreign Policy*, (Amritsar: Guru Nanak Dev University, 1983), pp. 319-320.
13. Kulwant Kaur, Pak-Afghan Relations, pp. 319-320.
14. Manan, Assessment of Afghan-Pak Relations, p. 28.
15. *Ibid.*, pp. 28-29.
16. Hafeez Malik, *Soviet Pakistan Relations and Post-Soviet Dynamics*, (London: The Macmilan Press, 1994), p. 126.
17. Ijaz Hussain, *Issues in Pakistan's Foreign Policy: An International Law Perspective*, (Lahore: Progressive Publishers, 1988), pp. 49-50, p. 155.
18. Kamal Matinuddin, *Power Struggle in the Hindu Kush: Afghanistan*, (1978-1991) (Lahore: Wajidalis Pvt. Ltd. 1991), p. 25.
19. Manan, Assessment of Afghan-Pak Relations, pp. 30-31.
20. Harvey, H. Smith et al, *Area Hand Book for Afghanistan*, (Foreign Area Studies: The American Universities, 1973), p. 223.
21. The New Times, 17 May 1970.
22. Malik, Soviet-Pakistan Relations and Post Soviet Dynamics, pp. 129-130.
23. Government of Pakistan, Background Information and Analysis: Pak-Afghan Relations (A General Survey) 1947-73, p. 19.
24. Ghaus, A.S., *The Fall of Afghanistan*, (Pergamon Brassy, International Defence Publisher, Washington D.C. 1988), p. 134.

CHAPTER-II

AFGHAN-PAK RELATION: BACKGROUND

Pakistan's Afghanistan Policy

Pakistan's foreign policy is economic and security driven since its inception in 1947. Therefore its foreign policy study remained a challenging subject for scholars. There is a great forbearance on its foreign policy in general and Afghan policy in particular, how it was created in 1947. They are the immediate neighbours having common border of 2240 kms long known as "Durand Line". The famous Indian poet, Mohammad Iqbal has rightly called Afghanistan as "the heart of Asia," while India's viceroy, Lord Curzon, called it the "Cockpit of Asia".[1] Pakistan considered Afghanistan as a potential friend in the region. Realising that landlocked Afghanistan was economically dependent on Pakistan, and given that both countries are Muslims.[2] Therefore, Pakistan assumed that it is a natural friend. Despite the geographic contiguity and shared borders, common faith and identities, the relations between two nations have not been so smooth. They have been engaged in conflicting interest with deep suspicions towards each other. Pakistan felt a security threat to its very existence due to fragile environment enveloping its East West borders which has been called "Pincer movement" by Ian Stephon.[3] Afghanistan has an irredentist claim to large parts of Pakistan, the so called Pukhtunistan issue.[4] Essentially, the Afghans argue that the Durand Line of 1893, which became Pakistan-Afghanistan border in 1947, was a British imposed colonial artefact that had lapsed with the demise of the British Indian Empire that created it.[5] The Durand Line separates the Afghan with Pakistani Pushtun populations. It is because of this rivalry Afghanistan was the only country to oppose newly independent Pakistan's membership in the United Nations in 1947.[6]

Pakistan and Afghanistan have historical threat perceptions from each other. They have been exploiting each other's vulnerabilities against each other. They have also been fearful and less at cooperation with each other.[7] Despite the impact and influence of volatile situations in Afghanistan over domestic politics of Pakistan, it has often decisively influenced the volatile security environment in Afghanistan.[8]

The intensity of hostility has been fluctuating with changing governments and regimes in both the nations. The feelings of estrangement have overshadowed the relations and prevented any consistent positive direction in their relations. However, during the monarchy regimes in Afghanistan the boundary and tribal ethnic issues were not provoked or intensified. They have developed distinct perceptions of regional roles and strategic visions became intermeshed in contending structures of power.[9]

Complicated and Multifaceted Relations

The regions that form contemporary Pakistan and Afghanistan share deep historical linkages. Even before the demarcation of the region as nation states, the territories of Pakistan and Afghanistan in ancient times were part of the great empires of the Persians, Greeks, Mauryas and Kushans. The Achaemenian Empire under Darius from (521 BC- 485 BC) held suzerainty over the area extending from Amu Darya (Oxus) to the banks of Indus. Later Alexander the Great conquered the Kabul valley and North West

Frontier Province in 327 BC.[10] Even under Ahmad Shah Abdali (Durrani), the founder of Afghanistan in 1747, his state included the areas of Punjab, Kashmir, Sind, Baluchistan, Balkh, Badakhshan and parts of Iranian Khorasan.[11]

On August 14, 1947, colonial rule over the Indian subcontinent ended with the creation of two separate states of India and Pakistan, carved out of Britain's Indian Empire. The newly formed government of Pakistan took control of the administration of the formerly British Indian provinces of Sind and NWFP. Baluchistan with its princely states of Kalat, Las Bela, Makran and Kharan also became part of West Pakistan. In the NWFP, Pakistan inherited the frontier tribal belt along with smaller Princely states of Dir, Amb, Swat and Chitral. The relations started deteriorating as the Afghan Government challenged the legality of NWFP's incorporation into the state of Pakistan. Afghanistan representative to the United Nations, Abdul Husain Khan Aziz, declared in September 1947 that his country did not recognise the NWFP as part of Pakistan and voted against Pakistan's membership in this organisation.[12] He said

> *We cannot recognise the North-West Frontier as part of Pakistan as long as the people of North-West Frontier have not been given an opportunity free from any kind of influence – and I repeat, free from any kind of influence – to determine for themselves whether they wish to be independent or to be become a part of Pakistan.*[13]

Even sometimes they demanded the amalgamation of Baluchistan with Afghanistan to gain the access to Arabian Sea.[14] Afghanistan's support for Pashtun irredentism, not only jeopardise the integrity of Pakistan but also challenged the very basic notion of Pakistani identity, which was being constructed on the basis of religious nationalism. Afghanistan put forward a demand for the creation of an independent "Pashtunistan," meaning "land of the Pashtuns."[15] The idea was that Pakistan should allow the Pashtuns in the northwestern part of their country to secede and become an independent state.[16] During that time the relations between Pakistan and Afghanistan have come to be centred on one issue. That issue was "Pashtunistan".[17] Pashtu's as a major ethnic group have been dominating the modern Afghan polity. They have established pastunwali or pakhtunwali as their code of honour and lived their life in accordance of this code.[18]

Historically, the NWFP was also Pashtu dominated region. Abdul Ghaffar Khan who is also known as Frontier Gandhi advocated a demand for independent *Pakhtunistan* in 1947. For this purpose he founded a movement called *Khudai Khidmatgar* (Servants of God).[19] However, after partition he forwarded demand for an autonomous *Pakhtunistan*.

Afghan government failed to negotiate with the British government on the issue of return of Pashtun territories in the months prior to the partition of India. This brought the Afghan rulers much closer to the *Khudai Khidmatgars* and motivated them to reject the Durand Line as the international frontier between Pakistan and Afghanistan. Pakistan held the view that it had inherited the rights over Pashtu territories as a successor to British India. Afghanistan has been refuting the treaties made during British India and claims to re-negotiate the Durand Line. However, Pakistan has shown disinterest in Afghan claims. Pakistan saw the Pashtunistan issue as an Afghan political manoeuvre aimed at destabilising Pakistan in the wake of Afghanistan's reluctance to have the validity of the Durand Line adjudicated by an international tribunal.[20] So this border dispute between Pakistan and Afghanistan made the chances of cooperation extremely difficult immediately after partition.

Although Pakistan and Afghanistan established diplomatic relations in February 1948 but the relations remained strained. However, the arrest of Khan Abdul Ghafar Khan has antagonised Afghanistan and in July 1949, the Afghan *Loya Jigra* revoked all the treaties, conventions and agreements signed with British, starting with the Durand Line Agreement. The Afghan government declared "Pashtunistan Day" as national holiday to be officially celebrated every year on August 31.[21] The relations were deteriorated more when the Pakistan Air Force bombed the village of Mogholgai, inside Afghanistan in June 1949.[22] Afghanistan discord with Pakistan over the status of the Frontier Province remained a central point in Afghan foreign policy from 1949-55. Afghanistan politicians and officials have raised the question regarding the safeguarding of the Pakistani Pashtuns in different International Organisations. Kabul sought support for its stance from virtually every major regional and extra-regional state.

Pakistan's Pro Western Approach and Afghan Reactions

By the late 1940's, Cold War between the United States led Western bloc and United Soviet Socialist Republic (USSR) led Eastern bloc entered into Pakistan-Afghanistan dispute. The newly independent states of Asia and Africa[23] became a battle ground upon which the geo-strategic and ideological competition between the US and Soviet Union was fought. In the post-Second War period, USA had tried to stop Soviet Union to fill the power vacuum[24] resulted by the collapse of British Empire.

The British withdrawal from India in 1947 and the partition of sub-continent had made the Afghans vulnerable. Afghanistan requested the loan of $100,000,000 to United States of America and was discussed in a conversation between the Director of National Economy and the Director General, Political Division, Ministry of Foreign Affairs of Afghanistan[25] and the American Minister and Secretary of Legislation in Afghanistan on April 25, 1946.[26] Abdul Majid Zabuli, the then Afghan Minister of National Economy visited Washington and pleads for arms supply from US in December 1948, to defend the Afghan territory in case of attack from USSR. However, United States negated the request of Afghanistan.[27] On the other hand the Soviet Union tried to strengthen its bilateral ties with Afghanistan which was started in early 1930's. On July 17, 1950, a Soviet-Afghan Trade Agreement was signed because Pakistan blocked trans-shipments of petroleum in 1950 for about three months, presumably as retaliation for tribal assaults across the border from Afghanistan.[28] Thus, Afghanistan was brought much closer to USSR.

Inspite of the strengthened relationship between Afghanistan and Soviet Union by the early 1950s, Kabul's ties with United States became increasingly complicated due to her soft attitude towards Pakistan in the Pashtunistan dispute. Although US rejected the Afghan request for military assistance because United State assumed that a large scale military assistance package might encourage Moscow to take overt action against that country,[29] Washington decided to extend technical assistance to Afghanistan under the Point Four Programme. US tried to bring cooperation between Pakistan and Afghanistan by offering them "Good Offices" in Novermber 1950, to deter Soviet designs in South Asia, but the dispute between these two countries became a hurdle for the United States to forge a solid anti-Soviet front in the region through the Cold War.[30]

In September 1953, King Muhammad Zahir's cousin and brother-in-law, Sardar Muhammad Daoud was appointed as Prime Minister of Afghanistan. The appointment of ambitious Daoud, who was formerly been the Minister of Defence, Commander of the Central forces in Kabul, would have important repercussions on the future course of the Pakistan-Afghanistan relations.[31] On the other hand Pakistan signed mutual support and defence agreement with United States in May 1954, which was not a military alliance, but marked the beginning of American arms sale to Pakistan, and an officer training project. In September 1954, Pakistan signed the Manila Pact, founding document of the Southeast Asia Treaty Organisation (SEATO).[32] On September 23, 1955 Pakistan joined the Baghdad Pact, which after Iraq withdrawal became Central Treaty Organisation (CENTO).[33] These treaties confirmed Pakistan's alliance with Washington.[34] In 1953-54, Daoud approached USA twice with a request for arms and economic assistance, and for an equitable resolution of the Afghan-Pakistan dispute.[35] So Daoud and his brother, Deputy Prime Minister and Foreign Minister Mohammad Naim, turned towards the Soviet Union in 1955 to seek much needed economic and military aid and established closer ties with Moscow to promote intensive internal economic development. USSR also found an opportunity in the shape of Afghanistan to check and exert pressure on neighbouring United States client states in the region, Iran and Pakistan. This decision of Daoud brought Afghanistan directly into the Cold War politics and gradually increased Soviet Union's influence in Afghanistan.[36]

In 1955, Pakistan decided to integrate all the four provinces of West Pakistan into one unit. Sardar Muhammad Daoud strongly protested against the "One Unit" scheme. There were demonstrations against the diplomatic missions of Afghanistan and Pakistan in Karachi and Kabul respectively.[37] People also attacked the Pakistani consulates in Kandahar and Jalalabad. Pakistan imposed economic blockade on Afghanistan and stopped the transit trade through the Khyber Pass and Karachi. Pakistan and Afghanistan broke off diplomatic relations and on October 13, 1955 Pakistan implemented the "One Unit" scheme in West Pakistan.[38] Pakistan also closed its consulates and trade establishments in Afghanistan.

Pakistan's border closure forced Daoud to request the Soviets for the renewal of 1950 transit and barter agreements. Soviet Prime Minister, Nikolai Bulganin and Nikita Khrushchev, First Secretary of the Central Committee of the Communist Party of the Soviet Union visited Afghanistan in December 1955 and granted US$100 million long-term development loan[39] to construct industrial and agricultural projects. In March 1956, various projects had been identified by joint Afghan-Soviet teams: Salang Tunnel through the Hindu Kush, two hydro-electric plants, a major air base in Bagram, three automotive repair and maintenance facilities, a road from Qazil Qala on the Iranian border to Kabul, three irrigation dams and canal systems, a fertiliser factory, and so on. The planning and implementation of these projects brought in large numbers of Soviet advisers and technicians. The Soviet economic penetration of Afghanistan had begun.[40] On the other hand Americans continued their low-level aid programme to Afghanistan and at the same time advised Iran and Pakistan to remain engaged with Kabul. Due to US efforts the relations between Afghanistan and Pakistan showed positive trend in 1956. Transit trade through Pakistan was resumed and Iskander Mirza, Pakistan President, visited Afghanistan in August 1956. In June 1957, Pakistani Prime Minister, Hussain Shaheed Surhrawardy held a meeting with Daoud in Kabul.

Military Intervention in Pakistan

Afghanistan-Pakistan relations entered into a new phase after the assumption of Power by Pakistani military under General Mohammad Khan in a *coup d'etat* in October 1958. General Khan was a Pashtun himself, belonged to the Hazara District of North West Frontier Province (now Khyber Pakhtunkhwa), but yet he had adopted a tougher stand on Afghanistan.[41] Relations between two countries deteriorated after the Pakistani military arrested two Pahtun leaders Abdul Ghaffar Khan and Abdul Samad Khan. Daoud quickly took action and informed Muhammad Hussain Maiwandwal, Afghan Ambassador to USA, to complain Mr. Rountree, Assistant Secretary of State for Near Eastern and South Asian Affairs, about the arrests. Maiwandwal said, He had received instructions from his government to bring to the attention of the United States Government the possible disturbing effect of recent developments in Pakistan on Afghanistan-Pakistan relations.[42]

Sardar Naim, Afghanistan Foreign Minister visited Pakistan in 1959, but General Ayub has warned him that

Pakistan can capture Kabul within hours, if the Afghanistan didn't stop their anti-Pakistan policy.[43] The relations deteriorated more in 1960 when the Nawab of Dir, a small princely state in the border area between Afghanistan and Pakistan, conspired with the Afghan government to secede from Pakistan and establish "the capital of free Pashtunistan" in Dir.[44] September 1960 saw the most serious fighting when Afghan tribesman and Afghan army regulars massed on the border to support the Nawab's secession. Pakistani army intervened to prevent it.[45] On September 6, 1960, Pakistan severed diplomatic relations with Afghanistan and halted all trade transit facilities. This hinders US aid projects in Afghanistan which were started to reduce Afghanistan dependence on Moscow. President Eisenhower sent special envoy, Livingston T. Merchant, to urge a peaceful resolution of tensions between Pakistan and Afghanistan. Merchant's mission failed to achieve any peace deal due to inflexibility of both the countries. During 1962 President Kennedy continued efforts for peace deal between these two neighbours. He requested Shah of Iran to mediate in the dispute.[46] Due to the economic blockade, the King and other members of the royal family thought that removal of the Prime Minister Daoud might lead to an improvement in relations with Pakistan and other Muslim states. Sardar Mohammad Daoud resigned on March 9, 1963 and Dr Mohammad Yousf became Prime Minister. Two months later, the Shah's mediatory efforts, backed by Washington got success and on May 26, 1963, Tehran Accord was signed. Pakistan and Afghanistan representatives agreed to restore diplomatic ties.[47]

Detent in Pakistan-Afghanistan Relations

A new constitution had been promulgated by the King Zahir Shah in 1964[48] and the political stability of Afghanistan rested on the equation established by him with the traditional leadership through such instrumentalities as the cabinet and parliament.[49] As the economic conditions in Afghanistan were deteriorating day by day, King tried to develop better relations with USA and Iran. There was improvement in relations between Pakistan and Afghanistan also. Afghanistan after the Daoud tenure paid only lip services for Pakhtunistan, however, it was not meant to their foreign policy during 1964-1972.

President Ayub visited twice in 1964 and again in 1966 to Afghanistan and the relation was cordial enough that Afghanistan kept quiet and did not create any trouble along Durand Line. In 1968, King Zahir Shah, visited Pakistan and received a very warm welcome.[50] On the other side, in Pakistan, due to pressure from popular demonstrations, President Ayub Khan resigned in March 1969. He handed over power to the Army Chief General Agha Muhammad Yahya Khan. Pakistan Finance Minister, Muzaffar Ali Khan visited Afghanistan as reciprocity to King's visit, to explore the possibilities of increasing trade and fields of economic cooperation.[51] The relations became more cordial when the Yahya Khan decided to disband the "One Unit Programme".[52] In October 1970, Pashtun leader Abdul Gaffar Khan was released.[53] These events help in increasing the economic cooperation and mutual understanding. The normalisation process starts gaining currency with every passing year.

On the other side of border, Yahya Khan hold's the Pakistan's first general elections in 1970, but it could not satisfy the Bengali people of East Pakistan, who where in majority in Pakistan and wanted their main political party "Awami League" who has won majority of the seats, to make government at the centre. This was acceptable neither to Yahya Khan and the army, nor to the Punjabi elites, nor to Bhutto, who demanded an equal share in government on the basis of his party's majority in West Pakistan. A series of moves and counter moves took place in the following months which results in the mass violent protests and clashes with the military in East Pakistan. Army launched "Operation Searchlight" on March 25, 1971 to suppress the people of East Pakistan.[54] On December 3, 1971, war between India and Pakistan broke out, and the Indian army made an incursion into East Bengal. The result was the emergence of another independent country in South Asia called Bangladesh. However, during the war period Afghanistan remained neutral and refrained from taking advantage of Pakistan's preoccupation in war.

Pakistan and Afghanistan before Soviet Intervention

Zulfikar Ali Bhutto, leader of the Pakistan People's Party (PPP), came to power in Pakistan, after Bangladesh creation.[55] Democratically elected government came into existence for the first time in Pakistan history.[56] He announced several changes in Pakistan's foreign policy to consolidate his power. The two major strands in his foreign policy perception were an emphasis on 'Third World Solidarity' and forging strong ties with Muslim states. However, Pakistan could form such strong ties with Afghanistan despite being a Muslim country because Afghanistan did not change its stand on Durand Line and continuously supported the 'self determination' of NWFP.

The separation of Bangladesh from Pakistan has changed the geo-political and geo-strategic culture of South Asian region. After Bangladesh liberation Afghanistan's geo-political and strategic importance has been felt very deeply by Pakistan. Therefore, Bhutto showed its keenness to forge cooperation with Afghanistan for the reason that Pakistan's defence priorities are attached with Afghanistan. However, Bhutto's discussions with King Zahir touched on Afghanistan's instigation of Pashtun nationalists in the Frontier Province. Even so, Bhutto got on well with the Afghan monarch and agreements were concluded on economic cooperation with Afghanistan.[57]

After the Simla Agreement of 1972 with India, Bhutto had changed his attitude towards NWFP and Baluchistan. He feared that the NAP leadership would join up with Afghanistan[58] and may support Pashtun and Baluch nationalism. By early 1973, the Federal government in

Islamabad began to show its uneasiness about Baluchistan government in stressing its demand for Provincial Autonomy. Islamabad alleged that Provincial government had failed to maintain law and order. Thus, Bhutto decided to dismiss the Baluchistan government on February 13, 1973. The coalition government in NWFP also resigned as a protest over this undemocratic action. The developments in Baluchistan and NWFP were a severe blow for the consolidation of democratic process in Pakistan after years of autocratic and repressive military rule.

As the central government was facing challenges in Pakistan, Sardar Mohammad Daoud deposed King Zahir Shah on July 17, 1973 in Afghanistan by a bloodless coup. King Zahir Shah was holidaying in Italy at the time of coup. Daoud declared himself President of the new Republic and announced the end of monarch. At his first press conference he said:

> *Whenever a nation verges on disaster and corruption in government institutions reaches its highest, and hope for reform is totally lost...then a resort to revolutionary reforms must take place.*[59]

The important role in the coup was played by *Parcham* of PDPA,[60] led by Karmal. Colonel Abdul Qadir, Head of the Air Force and the Commander of the Tank group in Kabul and Colonel Aslam Watanjar were the two key players in the coup and both were the members of Pro-Soviet PDPA's *Parcham* faction.[61] Besides declaring himself President and Prime Minister, Daoud also held the portfolios of foreign affairs and defence. He nominated 50 members Central Committee which includes the leading *Parcham* leaders like Babrak Karmal, Anahita Ratebzad and Noor Mohammad Noor. Numerous *Parchami* supporters were placed in the ministries and in the lower positions of the state bureaucracy.[62]

Daoud remained consistently advocating Pashtunistan even though he remained absent from active politics.

By keeping the Pashtunistan issue alive, he wants to unite the rivalry ridden Pashtu tribes situated on the sides of Durand Line. But this policy the non-Pashtun ethnic groups such as the Tajiks, Uzbeks, Hazaras began to challenge the Pashtu hold on power within Afghanistan. Different attempts were made to dislodge the Daoud regime, consecutively in September and December 1973 and June 1974.[63]

Daoud'd support for Pashtunistan had raised the anxieties of Bhutto. Bhutto believed that much of the tension in NWFP was due to the saboteurs trained by the Afghans. He insisted that the Afghan regime was behind all the troubles in the frontier state. The Pakistan government was angered with Afghan government providing sanctuary and financial assistance to Baluch separatists. So Bhutto started not just to neutralise the Afghan campaign but formulated a 'forward policy' to produce pressures within Afghanistan that could be used to reduce Daoud's urge to pursue the Pakhtunistan issue. An anti-Kabul propaganda centre whose goal was to destabilise Daoud's new regime was established in Pakistan. But Bhutto had more direct action in mind.[64]

Political Islamic movement led by religious intellectuals and scholars started in early 1970's. The leading figures in this movement were Professor Burhanuddin Rabbani and Professor Ghulam Muhammad Naizi, affiliated with Kabul University. Persons like Gulbuddin Hekmatyar, Ahmad Shah Masood, Abdul Haq and many others were part of this movement. Several important Pashtun Ulama and students such as Mawlawi Yunus Khalis, Muhammas Nabi Muhammad and Jalaluddin Haqqani were participated to this movement.[65] Bhutto got an opportunity and inspite of supporting the tribal dissidents in the border areas to counter Afghan irredentism; he provided protection as well as military training to Islamists in Afghanistan who's explicit was to overthrow the Daoud regime. In 1974, Professor Burhanuddin Rabbani and Gulbuddin Hekmatyar fled to Pakistan, Bhutto welcomed them, quickly recognising how these young activists and their followers could suit Pakistan's aims.[66]

Relations between Afghanistan and Pakistan deteriorated more during 1974-75. Afghanistan raised the issue of Pashtunistan in the UN General Assembly in an effort to obtain international support for it.[67] Daoud tried to pursue China to put pressure on Pakistan to settle the issue of Pakistan-Afghanistan. He also tried to get the assistance from Soviet Union and India against Pakistan.

On the other hand, Pakistan continued their assistance to Afghan Islamists. As Major General (retired) Naseerullah Babur said, between 1973-77 Pakistan army trained around 5000 Afghan Islamists.[68] In July 1975, Ahmad Shah Masood launched a full scale armed rebellion against Daoud regime. Gulbuddin Hekmatyar also planned an armed insurrection from Paktia province. But Afghan army successfully crushed the uprising by August 1975. The Kabul government used what means it had to aggravate political squabbles in Pakistan's NWFP. Bhutto also tried to make an alternate to the Daoud regime by using the services of ex-king Zahir Shah and formar Prime Minister, Musa Shafiq.

Daoud visited Moscow in June 1974 and subsequent visit of the Soviet President to Kabul in December 1975 has hardened the Daoud's stand on Pashtunistan.[69] On the other side Bhutto paid an official visit to Moscow on October 24-26, 1974.[70] Bhutto expressed Pakistan's interests in improving relations with Afghanistan. Soviet Union also wished the settlement of differences that became a hurdle in better relations. So Soviet Union decision of not supporting Afghanistan government on the issue of Pashtunistan was a positive sign.[71] Due to the soft attitude of the Soviet Union, in 1975, Daoud begun to significantly change the Afghan Foreign Policy. He initiated a policy of improving ties with neighbours particularly the Iran, Arab countries and China.

Afghanistan started developing good relations with Iran and in April 1975, Daoud visited Tehran. Iran offered economic agreement of US$ 2 billion over a period of ten years and a quick loan of US$ 400 million to finance development projects.[72] Mohammad Naim, brother of Doaud visited China in December 1974. As both Iran and China have cordial relations with Pakistan, it will have a positive impact on the future Afghanistan-Pakistan relations. The Iranian efforts and changes in foreign policy had helped Daoud to initiate negotiations with Pakistan in May 1975. Daoud and Bhutto held talks in Kabul during the latters visit to Kabul in the first week of June 1976.[73] Though neither side gave up its stand on the issues dividing them, but both governments recognised the need for goodwill to conduct negotiations and agreed that they would refrain from hostile propaganda against each other. Both agreed to solve their mutual problems on the basis of the five principles of peaceful[74] coexistence. In return Daoud visited Pakistan in August 1976 and stressed on the importance of Islamic brotherhood. This betterment in relations made Pakistan to stop their assistance to Afghan Islamists in early 1977.

Change of Leadership in Pakistan and Afghanistan

The normalisation of relations did not go smoothly. Negotiations were halted when Bhutto unexpectedly lost its legitimacy in the irregularities alleged in Pakistan's March 1977 National Assembly elections. By July 1977, after months of street demonstrations, the prime minister had been removed from his office by General Zia-ul-Haq. On January 7, 1977, Rafi Raza, a PPP leader (head of election campaign) announced that National Assembly elections would be held in March.[75] On January 11, 1977, nine Opposition parties[76] made a United Front called Pakistan National Alliance (PNA).[77] Their election manifestos were mainly on the grievances arising from inflation, government arbitrariness and unemployment. Although despite the PPP control of the media, use of machinery of government and intimidatory tactics, large crowds spontaneously flocked to PNA rallies. This feature of the campaign led most observers to anticipate a strong showing for the opposition, although no one doubted a PPP victory.[78]

In Late April 1977 panic striken Bhutto declared imposition of marshal law. Afghanistan looked 1977 military coup as internal matter of Pakistan and refrained from giving any comment on this development. Soon after the military regime had acquired the power in Pakistan and General Zia-ul-Haq continued the momentum in improving the Pakistan-Afghanistan relations that had development during the last years of Bhutto. General Zia informed Daoud that Pakistan wished not only to preserve the "Spirit of Kabul" but also to promote and strengthen it. He also expressed his desire to visit Kabul. Daoud in return invited General Zia to come to Afghanistan at his earliest convenience. The release of some of the Pashtun and Baloch leaders like Abdul Wali Khan, Sardar Khair Bux Marri, Ghaus Bux Bizenjo and Sardar Ataullah Mengal by Pakistan and appointment of Noor Ahmad Etemadi, a former Prime Minister, as Ambassador to Pakistan by Afghanistan were some of the positive developments. General Zia during a visit to Afghanistan in October 1977 developed a good understanding with Daoud. He invited President Daoud to visit Pakistan and the latter was agreed.[79] Daoud arrived in Islamabad on March 5, 1978 and held discussions with General Zia regarding further improvement in bilateral ties. Daoud said on March 8, 1978,

> *Pakistan and Afghanistan will now walk hand in hand in the warm glow of brotherhood...the era when both of us were subject to the old classic imperialist technique of 'divide and rule' is over.*[80]

The closeness of Pakistan and Afghanistan could not go long due to domestic problems in Afghanistan. Daoud had adopted the authoritarian methods to sustain his regime in power. He had not fulfilled the promises of good governance and social reforms. He also broke out the relations with *Parcham* group of PDPA that helped him to gain power in 1973. He replaced the old Constitution by his new "1977 Constitution" and formed uni-cameral legislature by replacing the existing bi-cameral legislature. These dictatorial methods had not only alienated both *Parcham* and *Khalq* groups of PDPA, but also the traditional clergy.

Daoud also had moved his regime away from Soviet influence by deepening relations with Iran and Muslim world. Iran's influence on Afghanistan was increasing day by day. Even Iran's intelligence agency started giving training to Afghan secret policy. Daoud's visit to Saudi Arabia and Egypt had helped him to get closer to Muslim world. So Daoud growing relations with Muslim world and West had increased Soviet Union apprehensions about the future Soviet – Afghanistan relations. Due to these circumstances the *Khalq* and *Parcham* factions of PDPA agreed to unite in 1977, following persistent pressure from the Soviet Union.[81]

The PDPA's unity move was in fact aimed to deter the Daoud's policy of moving away from Soviet Union. During the early days of 1978 Daoud's popularity has declined because of his dictatorial policies and ailing economy. On April 17, 1978 Mir Akbar Khybar, the founder of the PDPA and a well known *Parcham* leader was assassinated.[82] Different theories were put forward about the death of Khyber. The PDPA alleged that Khybar was killed on the orders of Daoud's interior minister,[83] Abdul Qadir Nuristani, who had been assumed to be influenced by SAVAK[84] against communists. However Daoud blamed the *Khalq* faction for the killing. There were massive demonstrations in Kabul against the killing of Khybar.[85] In this connection, the *Khalq* and *Parcham* of PDPA organised demonstrations against Doaud regime. In return most of the Communist leaders were either arrested or kept under close scrutiny by Daoud regime.[86] The principal leaders like Nur Mohammad Taraki, Hafizullah Amin and Babrak Karmal were kept under house arrest.[87] However, Hafizullah Amin organised the coup at his home with support of policemen.[88] On the morning of April 27, 1978, Presidential palace was attacked with a small group of military officers[89] from Fourth Armored Corp and

Air Force. The attack was led by Colonel Abdul Qadir, Vice Commander of the Air Force, and by Major Aslam Watanyar. Daoud Palace Guards, equipped with tanks and armoured personnel carriers, defended the Presidential Palace for several hours amidst MiG 21s.[90] But by the evening Daoud and about thirty of his relatives had been executed. The people of Afghanistan then heard over Radio Kabul that a "Revolutionary Council" headed by Taraki had taken charge.[91] This coup was named as *Saur*[92] Revolution of 1978. On April 30, 1978, the Republic of Afghanistan was renamed the Democratic Republic of Afghanistan (DRA).[93]

The new power edifice, quickly assembled by the party, was a three tier hierarchy with overlapping membership: the central committee at the top, a 35-member Revolutionary Council at the middle level, and a 21-member Cabinet for day to day administration.[94]

The Saur Coup had a very deep impact on Pakistan. During the time of coup the Zia administration in Pakistan was in the process of imposing an Islamisation agenda to counter the leftist opposition led by Bhutto's Pakistan People's Party. Military regarded the change in government in Kabul as a Soviet inspired move that threatens the Pakistan Security. Pakistan army regarded the leftist coup in Kabul as threatening and a potential threat for the fragile military regime.[95] For Zia-ul-Haq, a follower of the Islamic teachings of Jammat-i-Islami founder Syed Abul Ala' Mawdudi, a Marxist regime in Afghanistan was certainly a matter of tension. In this regard, Zia-ul-Haq issued a warning to Pakistan's 'leftists' after the Saur coup to behave or face the consequences. He observed that: 'the sooner the leftist wake up and come to the middle of the road, the better it would be for them'.[96]

Zia-ul-Haq, immediately after the change of government in Kabul, called the special cabinet meeting to discuss Pakistan's future policy towards Afghanistan. Lietenant General Faiz Ali Chisti, an important member of the meeting stressed that Pakistan should adopt a forward policy and install a favourable government in Kabul with the help of Pashtun tribes. Inspite of the apprehensions about the new regime, on May 5, 1978, Pakistan recognised the newly named "Democratic Republic of Afghanistan" after consulting its major allies, United States, Iran and Saudi Arabia and maintained diplomatic relations with it. Due to the communist regime in Kabul, Pakistan started support to Afghan resistance, popularly known as Mujahideen.[97]

In September 1978, General Zia-ul-Haq met President Nur Mohammad Taraki, both leaders saw the contrast in their fundamental beliefs. General Arif wrote, "the two Muslims disagreed on the interpretation of Islamic philosophy".[98] Taraki told Zia that the Afghan royal family "had exploited the Afghan nation for 200 years. Now everything belongs to people. The revolution has given land to eleven million people". Zia responded that "Muslims must consider all property as belongings to Allah and should see man only as His custodian". Taraki responded, "All land belongs to the tiller". Zia's invitation "to be fearful of God and to recognise obligations towards God" were met with Taraki's comment that, "God is *aadil* (just). We don't have to fear a just God."

Zia-ul-Haq's military regime had apprehensions that Taraki will revive the Pashtunistan issue. These apprehensions turned into reality when the President of Afghanistan met with Abdul Ghaffar Khan May 1978 and raised the border issue with Pakistan. The PDPA's stance on the Pakistani Pashtun and Baluch problem signaled the renewal of tensions between Kabul and Islamabad.[99]

PDPA regime had signed some 30 agreements with in six months of the coup worth more than US$14 billion, with Soviet Union and other Eastern bloc countries in the areas of defence, culture, education and health. Particularly important were those for the additional cooperation for oil and gas and for the building of a linking road and rail bridge and associated communication system across the Oxus at Hairatan.[100] These agreements had strengthened the Soviet

Union hold on Afghan economy. Pakistan fears that this Afghan socialist model could affect the Baluch and Pashtun minorities. Also in May-June 1978 PDPA regime announced number of radical social and economic reforms like land reforms, improvement in the status of women, alleviating the 90 per cent illiteracy rate, granting rights to minorities. It has also helped in cancellation of peasant debts owed to rich landlords. All of these measures would have seriously undermined the privileges of the exclusively male, conservative and primitively Muslim leaders of the rural communities.[101]

PDPA announced socio-political reforms in its agenda of equal rights for men and women and status of national language to Nuristani, Uzbek and Turkmen. This resulted in Pashtu revolt in Kunar valley, Badakshan and Hindu Kush. The government's mass arrests further alienated the opposition groups. These rebellious groups established contacts with Zia government in Pakistan.[102]

These policies forced many tribal chiefs and their followers to move into Pakistan where they were received with open arms by the Zia regime. Every arriving Afghan was given four rupees as a daily stipend of– more than the average income of an Afghan peasant. According to governmental references, around 18,000 Afghan refugees had arrived in Pakistan during 1978 and for humanitarian assistance around 145 million dollars have been spend on refugees acclaimed by Pakistan.[103] The situation in Afghanistan prompted General Zia to organise the disparate Afghan Islamic groups in Pakistan into a viable political and military force under Pakistani control. This policy domestically assisted the Pakistani military regime in giving legitimacy to its Islamic credentials. On the other hand PDPA regime's reliance on the USSR found reflections in a treaty of Friendship and Cooperation,[104] signed by Brezhnev and Taraki on December 5, 1978.

Under these circumstances different Afghan groups presented a colour of unity under the tutelage of the

Pakistani military in order to get Western support. Seven major Afghan Islamic parties gained prominence in the West with the support of Zia-ul-Haq regime. They were together called Islamic Union of Afghan Mujahideen. The main parties were:

1. *Jamiat-i-Islami-i-Afghanistan,* (JIA), i.e. *Islamic Society of Pakistan,*[105] headed by Professor Burhanuddin Rabbani. It had established in Pakistan in 1974. Its famous guerrilla commander was Ahmad Shah Masood.
2. *Hizb-i-Islami* i.e. *Party of Islam* headed by Gulbuddin Hekmatyar. Hekmatyar was openly supported i.e. *The National Islamic Front of Afghanistan* headed by Pir Syed Ahmad Gaylani. It's office by the leaders of the Pakistani Jamaat-i-Islami.[106]
3. *Hizb-i-Islami* i.e. *Party of Islam* headed by Mawlawi Muhammad Yunus Khalis was founded in 1979. The Khalis group's military commander, Jalaluddin Haqqani gained prominence against Soviet forces during 1980's.[107]
4. *Jabha-i-Nejat-i-Melli-i-Afghanistan* i.e. *National Front for the salvation of Afghanistan* headed by Sibghatullah Majaddidi. It had established its office in Peshawar in June 1978.
5. *Harakat-i-Inqilab-i-Islam* i.e. *Islamic Revolutionary Movement* headed by Mawlawi Muhammad Nabi Muhammadi. It had established its office in Quetta in late 1978.[108]
6. *Mahaz-i-Melli-i-Islami-i-Afghanistan* was established in Peshawar in August 1978.
7. *Ittehad-i-Islam* i.e. *Islamic Unity* led by former theology lecturer of Kabul University, Abdur Rab Rasul Sayyaf. It was formed in early 1979.[109]

Pakistan gave substantial financial and military aid to these Afghan-based Mujahideen groups. Pakistani bases used for training and facilitation incursions in Afghanistan were located in different area of NWFP[110], Baluchistan[111] and Punjab.[112, 113] On the other side of the border, in Afghanistan, rivalry between *Khalq* and *Parcham* were increasing day by day.[114] President Taraki's Deputy Prime Minister, Hafizullah Amin, enhanced his power base in 1979. Taraki died in such circumstances which aroused an assumption that it was a political murder.[115]

With the elimination of Taraki, the increased instability in Afghanistan gave an impetus to the Pakistani military to weaken the PDPA's hold on power. By September 1979, fighting in eastern Afghanistan resulted in increasing the number of refugees in Pakistan to 170,000.[116] The Zia regime's strategy found a sympathetic ally in the Carter administration. The growing armed opposition in Afghanistan from September to December 1979 substantially reduced PDPA control over large parts of the country. Pakistan's enhanced role in backing this increasingly Islamic oriented insurgency during this period had the consent of the United States.

After becoming the President of Democratic Republic of Afghanistan, Hafizullah Amin earned the support of the Soviet Union. But the Soviet did not approve the actions of the Amin which were alienating the Afghans from the pro-Marxist PDPA. Although Amin was totally dependent on the Soviet for political, economic and military support, he wants to act independently. Even he refused to visit Moscow. These independent acts of Amin challenged the Soviet Union's investment and strategic interests. Inspite of the Soviet pressure, he began his one man rule.

He took initiatives to revive friendly ties with Pakistan. But Pakistan continued its support for the Peshawar-based Islamic parties, although the material support was very minimal at this stage, compared to the levels that were to be reached after the Soviet invasion. Amin was considering a trade off: Afghan acceptance of the Durand Line as an international frontier in return for an end to Pakistani support of the regime's enemies. He extends an invitation to Zia-ul-Haq to send his foreign minister, Agha Shahi, to Kabul. Shahi's planned to visit Kabul on 22 December 1979, but could not materialise due to Soviet invasion to Afghanistan.[117]

At the same time, Amin initiated some overtures to the US with whom relations had become soured since the Dubs episode[118] and the suspension of the US assistance programmes. Some US diplomatic contacts with Amin had taken place in the autumn but nothing had come of them. But in home, a serious opposition and armed resistance was gaining momentum because of his policies. By the October 1979, the question was only, who would replace him, the Mujahideen or the Soviets.

Soviet Intervention

The Soviet invasion came into Afghanistan in spring of 1979 in the backdrop of dwindling political in Afghanistan.[119] From late November 1979, the Soviet troops began to move. A 1500 man heavily equipped airborne division was gradually flown from the Tajik Soviet Socialist Republic to Bagram Air Base and Soviet infantry and armoured battalions were moved to Kabul Airport. On December 20, another armoured unit took over the Salang Tunnel to protect the key land link between Kabul and the Amu Darya border.[120] These careful preparations assured a smooth and relative painless invasion. On December 25, 1979, when whole world was celebrating the Christmas, Soviet ground forces entered Afghanistan via Turkmenistan and Uzbekistan. Airborne troops landed in Herat, Kandhar and Jalalabad. By the 27th, there were 50,000 Soviet troops in Afghanistan.[121]

Soviet troops seized radio station after disabling the telephone network in Kabul. Darul Aman Palace was surrounded by other forces where Amin was hiding. In a close fighting, Amin was killed. Those of the 1800 Afghan guards who survived the fighting were reportedly executed. Babrak Karmal announced on December 27, at 8:45 PM that he had put an end to the "intolerable violence and torture of the bloody apparatus of Hafizullah Amin" by deposing the rogue. Karmal was appointed as Prime Minister, President, and Secretary General of the PDPA. On the morning of 28th December, Kabul Radio announced that the new government had appealed for assistance, including military aid, from the Soviet Union under the 1978 Friendship Treaty,[122] in response to provocations by foreign enemies. Karmal himself did not appear in the country until January 1, 1980.[123]

US President Jimmy Carter called the attack "an extremely serious threat to peace" and "a violation of the United Nations Charter." This forced Jimmy Carter to enunciate 'Carter Doctrine' in his state of the Union Address on January 23, 1980. He said,

> *Let our position be absolutely clear: An attempt by any outside force to gain control of the Persian Gulf region will be regarded as an assault on the vital interests of the United States of America, and such an assault will be repelled by any means necessary, including military force.*[124]

US openly come out in support of the Mujahideen groups, whose struggle was now called 'Jihad' against Communism. Soviet intervention was visualised by US foreign policy elites as a part of the Soviet grand strategy to expand its influence up to warm waters of the Arabian Sea and Persian Gulf.[125]

The entry of Russian troops into Afghanistan has changed the political structure of whole region. Although Pakistan was under threat having a direct border with Soviet Union, the military regime got an opportunity to gain popular support. Zia-ul-Haq, gave an impression to the US that he was fearful of the Soviet threat to Pakistan. He said that Vietnam like situation can be created for the Soviets, but for that US would have to commit itself for security of Pakistan. The then US security advisor Zbigniew Brzezinski publicly assured its support for Pakistan. He has also rejuvenated Mutual Defence Treaty of 1959, which says US will aid Pakistan in case of Communist attack.[126]

Meanwhile, after rejecting the Carter Administration's offer of US$ 400 million by Zia-ul-Haq in January 1980, in September 1981, the new US administration provided US$7.2 billion worth of military and economic assistance for over twelve years. The US supplied the sophisticated military hardware like forty F-16 jet and provided training and education to the Pakistani military officers.[127]

Pakistan also skillfully utilised International Organisations like OIC, NAM and the UN to harness the sympathy of the international community for its stance on the Afghan issue and helped to get economic support from Western and Arab countries. On the other side of the coin, the Afghan Jihad was at core of Zia's policies to consolidate his power. After receiving the large sums of aid money from USA and other countries, Pakistan increased dramatically the quantity and quality of support for the Mujahedeen groups. The refugee camps of Afghan people in Pakistan became an important base for Jihadi recruitments.[128]

Zia-ul-Haq in collaboration with CIA allowed thousands of Arab volunteers coming from Egypt, Saudi Arabia, the Gulf Sheikhdoms, Iraq, Algeria, Jordan, Syria, and even the Israeli occupied Arab territories to enter Pakistan and join the anti-Soviet struggle. These Arab countries also provide financial assistance of US$5 billion to Afghan resistance during 1986-1990.[129] In addition to the overt and covert funding operation by several Western and Arab governmental agencies for the Mujahedeen, a plethora of private aid agencies, think tanks and other outfits opened offices in Pakistan, with the apparent aim of liberating Afghanistan from the clutches of the Soviets.

The Arab States also set up a vast array of welfare and relief agencies for the Afghans in Pakistan. The Saudis were most active in establishing their governmental and non-governmental organisations in NWFP and Baluchistan. Saudi Red Crescent opened its office in 1980 and Saudi Relief Committee, Kuwait Red Crescent and Islamic Relief Agency of Sudan opened their offices during 1981-85. In 1984, Osama Bin Laden opened the *Maktab al Khidmat lil Mujahedeen* or the Services Office for the Mujahedeen in Peshawar with the help of the Saudi Intelligence Chief, Prince Turki bin Faysal bin Abdul Aziz, and the Pakistani ISI.[130] Soon several other Arab non-governmental agencies, like Afghanistan Reconstruction Office funded by King Fahd, The Education Centre funded by Egyptian Sheikh Fathi Al Refai opened their offices in Peshawar. These Islamic NGOs with substantial support from their governments developed linkages with Pakistani and Afghan Islamic parties.

Fragile Alliance of Resistance Forces

In 1980, the government of Pakistan gave formal recognition to seven political parties headquartered in Peshawar, in response to pressures to raise the international profile of the Afghan resistance. The people of Afghanistan have to register with any of seven parties to receive Pakistani aid otherwise he will get nothing, no arms, no ammunition and no training. Most of the military and financial aid from Pakistan, the United States, Saudi Arabia and other interested foreign parties was funneled through these seven groups, although smaller factions continued to compete for such support as well. Membership in these groups was fluid, and alliances came and went during the years of struggle. Still other, unaffiliated groups fought from bases within the country.[131] By the end of 1981, the number of resistance groups exceeds forty. Resistance activity inside Afghanistan had developed simultaneously and its coordination and effectiveness had correspondingly begun to depend on organised parties to discharge logistical functions. There were reports of fighting among contending Mujahideen groups and interdiction of supplies.[132] The Shia groups were confined to Afghanistan, received aid and support from Iran. The Sunni resistance groups were backed by Pakistan.

Following the unsuccessful attempts to build an alliance in 1981 and 1982, the Peshawar based parties remained divided along fundamentalist (Haftagan) and moderate (Sehgan) lines for most of 1983 and 1984. The animosity was so deep that the two groups could not agree on a spokesman to deliver a statement on behalf of Afghan resistance, at the August 1982, Islamic Foreign Ministers Conference at Niamey, capital of an African country, Niger. Both groups separately meet the Pakistan Foreign Minister, Shabzada Yaqub Khan, staking their claims to represent the Afghan Mujahideen. Because of this fragile nature, there was no delegation representing the resistance in New York at the time of the United Nations General Assembly debate on Afghanistan in 1982-84. The parties remained unrepresented at other International Conferences.[133] In addition to ideological divisions, rivalries ran through the Afghan Mujahideen along ethnic, tribal and personal lines, e.g. there were instances of hostility between Ahmad Shah Masood and Gulbuddin Hekmatyar.

But the situation starts changing by the end of 1984, when it appeared that greater coordination among the Mujahideen groups and a united front for the Peshawar based parties would help in projecting resistance internationally. The new seven party alliance, called the Islamic Unity for Afghan Mujahideen (IUAM), but usually referred to as the Afghan Alliance, was established in May 1985 with direct intercession from Zia-ul-Haq. It was decided that Afghan Alliance would have a different spokesman every three months, on a rotating bases. Three months later, the Alliance announced a twenty one member "supreme council" or "Shura," to direct the jihad inside Afghanistan.[134] This helped to solve the problem to some extent as after 1985, Mujahideen groups were represented at regular basis by its current spokesman at Geneva, New York and elsewhere but some independent parties still continue to work independently.

The War and Zia-ul-Haq's Diplomacy of Survival

Pakistan became the frontline state against the Soviet dominated Afghanistan. Zia-ul-Haq used the Afghan card in the power game to his best advantage, and profited from the Afghan conflict to bolster his armed forces more effectively than ever. His Afghan policy was not dictated by Islamic fraternity alone. He saw that channeling arms towards the mujahedeen would give him a unique opportunity to ensure that he had a say in the choice of future leaders of a country that had been a difficult neighbour for so long, but one which, once an ally - even a protected one – would obtain for Pakistan the strategic depth it needed to confront India.[135] Zia was equally determined to outdo the Soviet and Indian influence in its immediate neighbouring country. In this connection Pakistan tried to have a friendly or a puppet government in Afghanistan. He clearly outlined his stance to a American journalist Selig Harrison:

> *We have earned the right to have a friendly government in Kabul. We won't permit it to be like it was before, with Indian and Soviet influence there and claims to our territory. It will be the real Islamic state, part of a pan-Islamic revival, that will one day win over the Muslims in the Soviet Union, you will see.*[136]

The first five years of Afghan resistance i.e. 1980-85 had swung the mood in the United States decisively in favour of a strong US commitment to help the Afghan resistance. The unwritten Reagan Doctrine to support anti-communist guerrilla movements and "roll back" Soviet advances of the 1970's had become fully operative. In late 1984 the bleeders began to push successfully for a major escalation of American weapons aid to the resistance. Congress overwhelmingly approved a resolution calling for more and better aid and in April 1985 President Ronald Reagan pushed through National Security Directive 166, which outlined plans for driving forces of Soviet Union from Afghanistan "by all means available." Therefore, US increased its aid from $120, $250, $470 and $630 million in 1984, 1985, 1986, and 1987 respectively.[137] US provided huge aid to Pakistan also and provided F16 aircraft jets. The then undersecretary of state James Buckley explained to *The New York Times* that such our aid and support to Pakistan would address "the underlying sources of insecurity that prompt a nation like Pakistan to seek a nuclear capability in the first place." In 1983, Pakistan received first fighter jet from US.[138]

The Pakistani military elite under Zia had artfully used the Soviet threat to expand the armed forces and assured their overbearing influence on the political system of the country. The situation in Afghanistan helped Zia to perpetually execute martial law. The US support also legitimised his military dictatorship to trample down democratic institutions and aspirations of the Pakistan. He was able to suppress opposition parties and postpone elections indefinitely. The US financial and military largesse emboldened the military junta in creating a pan-Islamic militant movement that could serve Islamabad's long-term geo-strategic objectives in South and Southwestern Asia. Most significantly, this policy enabled Zia to firmly establish the armed forces as the only body that could guard Pakistan's 'ideological' and 'geographical' frontiers.[139] The 'army' and 'Islam' became synonymous for the preservation of Pakistan's national integrity. Zia saw himself as divinely ordained to preserve Pakistan's Islamic identity.[140] In short, while preserving his own image, he destroyed the democratic institutions.

The Geneva Negotiations and Soviet Withdrawal

Almost eight years of civil war and foreign military intervention in Afghanistan had resulted in terrible loss of human life and massive physical destruction. While headlines focused on the war, the UN settlement had slowly been taking shape behind the scenes since 1982. Each step forward in the Geneva negotiations strengthened the forces in Moscow favouring disengagement. However, the historical evidence available so far appears that as early as May 1980, Moscow and Kabul made their first formal overtures for negotiations. Pakistan rejected demands for a direct government-to-government dialogue that would have implied recognition of the Kabul regime because in the tense Cold War atmosphere, the US reportedly put pressure on the Zia regime to refrain from giving in to Soviet overtures for a negotiated settlement of the Afghan issue. Instead, Pakistan Foreign Minister Agha Shahi insisted on a UN sponsored dialogue in which Kabul would not be represented by the government.[141] By January 1981, Soviet dropped the demand for direct government-to-government exchanges and agreed that the UN could play a defined role.[142]

Encouraged by Shahi and Soviets, then UN Secretary General Kurt Waldheim sent Javier Perez de Cuellar[143], at that time undersecretary general for special political affairs, on two missions to Kabul, Islamabad and Tehran in 1981. Perez de Cuellar said, "The Russian want to do something, but Kabul is nervous. What we have is a bridge of straw, and we shouldn't try to run across it too much." Soon after becoming secretary general in January 1982, Perez de Cuellar appointed Cordovez, who flew to Islamabad and Kabul in April to prepare the ground for what was to be the first 12 rounds of negotiations in Geneva that June.[144] The external environment was not conducive to progress in the negotiations because Soviets had become deeply embroiled in Afghanistan and Washington showed little enthusiasm for negotiations.[145]

Cordovez shuttled between Kabul and Islamabad for 17 days in late January and early February 1983. When he returned, he was ready to put together his "first real draft, the first unified, completed text" of the projected agreement. Kabul had accepted the language of the first section, including a time frame clause, and Islamabad had agreed that the second section would contain mutual pledges of non-interference. However, despite the uneven progress on the draft texts, the April 11-22, 1983 round talks was suspended on an optimistic note, to be resumed in late June 1983. The aftermath of the April round was marked by expressions of optimism from UN and Pakistani sources. Upto this time, Moscow had never made a public commitment about the withdrawal, but on May 19, then Soviet Ambassador to Pakistan, Vitaly Smirnov, publically confirmed Kabul's "willingness to give a timetable for the withdrawal of the total Soviet contingent."[146] However, hopes for a break-through quickly evaporated at the June round amid mutual accusations. Soviet negotiator at Geneva, Vasily Safronchuk, told Cordovez that Moscow did not regard Pakistan as a free agent in the negotiations.[147]

After the June session, the negotiating process shifted into slow gear. Only after a gap of more than one year was the next round, convened, from August 23-30, 1984. During this round Pakistan agreed to begin discussions on a non-interference treaty. Privately, Pakistan Foreign Minister, Sahebzada Yakub Khan, also accepted the Cordovez compromise on the timing of the aid cutoff: the treaty would go into effect at the same time as the start of the withdrawal. Later attacked by critics as the "Day One" formula, this provision was not accepted by Moscow until mid-1985. Islamabad coupled its shift on the treaty with a demand for parallel negotiations on a withdrawal agreement to be signed by Moscow as well as Kabul. Until then Moscow had argued that Soviet troops had been invited to intervene; therefore, the Soviet commitment to withdraw would be made only to Afghanistan. Kabul, in turn, would confirm the withdrawal of "foreign troops" in its agreement with Islamabad. Moscow and Kabul flatly rejected the Pakistani demand, insisting that they would discuss the withdrawal only in direct talks.[148]

Significantly, the advent of Mikhail Gorbachev as General Secretary of the Communist Party of Soviet Union (CPSU) Central Committee[149] in 1985 heralded dramatic changes in Soviet foreign policy, aimed at reducing tensions with the US Gorbachev opened new channels with the US for the resolution of the Afghan conflict. Gorbachev supported the Geneva process and accepted the role of the UN. So, the fifth Geneva round was held in June 1985. It began with the usual overture: Pakistan stressing discussion on time frame, Cordovez Pushing for the finalisation of the text, and the Afghans and Soviets refusing to deal with the issue of withdrawal in a manner that would legally appear to commit them to Pakistan or the United States. The Afghan side refused to consider either the text or the format and instead demanded vigorously for direct talks.

The Sixth and Seventh rounds of Geneva negotiations convened on August 27-39, 1985 and December 16-19, 1985 respectively. Both the rounds remained preoccupied with the issue of direct talks and the related questions about the procedures and understandings needed to initiate discussion. The year 1986 brought fourth increasingly visible signs of Soviet difficulties in Afghanistan and Soviet desire for a political settlement. The most significant indication came in Gorbachev's famous statement when he described Afghanistan as a "bleeding wound" while addressing to the 27th Soviet Communist Party Congress on February 26, 1986. The eighth round was the single longest round, lasting from May 5-23, 1986. It was spent mostly on cleaning up the text of instrument IV and various auxiliary issues, while waiting for a time frame offer from the Soviet-Afghan side. The ninth round of talks held in August 1986 did not produce anything significant.

The tenth round of talks was convened from February 25 to March 9, 1987. Cordovez convened to the interlocutors that this round would be focused on time frame, which he intended to finalise no matter how long the two delegations had to stay at Geneva. The Geneva round started with routine posturing. The two sides were locked into bargaining on the time frame. The Afghanistan delegation finally offered eighteen months time frame while Pakistan signaled its readiness to accept seven month. In September 1987, amid Soviet hints that a major timetable concession would be forthcoming, Kabul asked Cordovez to convene an eleventh Geneva round. The Afghans came with a new figure of sixteen months, a reduction of two months from their previous offer of eighteen months. On the other side Pakistan Foreign Minister Yaqub Khan raised the figure offered by

Pakistan to eight months. In November 1987, Soviet official spokesman Gennadi Gerasimov remarked that it would be possible for the Soviet Union to withdraw in seven to twelve months, although he still seemed to link the decision to reconciliation.[150] Finally, at the Washington Summit, December 8-10, 1987, Gorbachev disclosed to the US side the new Soviet position on the time frame and the Geneva settlement, and made public at the conclusion of the summit. In a statement to the press in Washington on December 10, Gorbachev announced Soviet willingness to offer a twelve month time frame, provided there was an agreement on cessation of "military and financial" assistance to the mujahedeen. Retreating the Soviet desire to see a nonaligned, neutral Afghanistan, Gorbachev stated that Moscow was not trying for a pro-Soviet government in Kabul and, similarly, Washington should not strive for a pro-US government.[151]

The position taken by the Soviets at the Washington summit cleared the way for the Geneva settlement. There was little left to discuss in the context of the four instruments except whether the Soviets could offer an even shorter time frame and agree to frontloading as provided in the text. The different reactions by Zia-ul-Haq and Junejo to Gorbachev's declaration foreshadowed the political wrangles that dominated the final phase of the negotiations. Gorbachev again moved to bring the Geneva process to a head by setting dates and cutting through the confusion surrounding a precise time frame and terminal date for withdrawal. In a statement telecast from Moscow on February 8, Gorbachev offered to withdraw Soviet troops beginning 15 May and ending ten months later, provided a Geneva settlement was concluded on March 15, 1988. The time frame was without any precondition of national reconciliation. Gorbachev's statement forced Pakistan to face the stark choice of signing or not signing the Geneva settlement. This became the focal point of diplomatic and political activity germane to the Afghan issue.

The principal factor accelerating the pace towards the Geneva settlement in the first week of April 1988 was the Soviet resolve to pull out of Afghanistan without further delay. The Soviets keenly desired the Geneva Accords because they provided the Soviets a neat and honourable framework to affect withdrawal from Afghanistan. On the face of it, according to the agreements, the Soviet Union was undertaking withdrawal in return for a commitment and guarantees on non-interference in the internal affairs of Afghanistan. In any event, if Pakistan were to continue to supply arms to the resistance, Moscow and Kabul could enjoy the propaganda advantage of accusing Pakistan of violating the Accords. The stage was thus set for the signing of the Geneva Accord. In a press conference on April 8, 1988 Cordovez promptly scheduled the ceremony for 14 April.

Almost one week was spent in attending to the technical details of translation and mutual authentication of texts, which were provided in Pashto, Urdu, and Russian, in addition to the English version. There were also a plethora of minor issues of practice and procedure relating to the use of national paper, folders, ribbons, seals and the shape of the table, which were solved before the grand day. The signing ceremony was a grand occasion for the United Nations. Finally the agreement was concluded on April 14, 1988 by the foreign minister of Afghanistan, Abdul Wakil, Pakistan's Foreign Minister, Zail Noorani, the Soviet Union representative, Eduard Shevardnade and the United States representative, George Shultz called for the complete withdrawal of Soviet forces.

Post Geneva Scenario

On May 15, 1988, the day the Geneva accords entered into force, with this Soviet withdrawal process started in presence of UN forces. These troops evacuated via Kabul to Khairkhana and Khairatan and crossed the border on May 19.[152] But the process of withdrawal was hardly a smooth process. Nijibullah seems to have little faith at all that his regime would survive. On April 28, he stated, probably more out of hope than conviction that Soviet military advisers would remain in Afghanistan after the withdrawal. In June he visited Moscow and met Gorbachev. Anatoly Chernyaev mentioned that during the meeting Gorbachev tried to impress upon Najibullah the concept for withdrawal, but the Najibullah acted desperate. Najibullah proposed to organise a campaign collectively with USSR and India against Pakistan. However, Gorbachev ridiculed the options.[153]

Besides this, Moscow continued to pressurise the USA and Pakistan over their support for the resistance. Only July 23, Soviet Deputy Foreign Minister Vladimir Petrovskii in an interview with *The Washington Post* warned that the withdrawal might not meet the 15 February deadline unless aid to the Mujahedeen was cut off. And on August 7, Moscow threatened counteraction against Pakistan if 'crude violations' of the Geneva Accords continued.[154] Even at one time Soviet Union announced suspension of the withdrawal. But according to Barnett Rubin, in all this there was a large dose of bluff, because it remained fundamentally in the Soviet Union's interest to extract itself from Afghanistan, whether Najibullah survived or not.[155]

As the final date for the withdrawal approached, the Kabul regime becomes more and more isolated. In the first week of January 1989, the Soviets closed their military hospital in Kabul and evacuated the patients. On January 21, West Germany's diplomatic personel left, and on January 27, the United Kingdom, France, Japan, and Italy announced that they were withdrawing their diplomats. Finally, on January 30, the US formally closed its Embassy. Finally on February 14, 1989, the last Soviet tank crossed the Hairatan Bridge over the Amu Darya, thus completed the withdrawal of Soviet troops from Afghanistan.

The end of the Soviet involvement saw different illegitimate or enfeebled claimants to power pitted against each other, in a country whose 'state' had limited capacity to function autonomously without external baking.

The Najibullah regime was challenged at the political level by the impotent interim Islamic Government and its self-interested external promoters. The significant legitimate power of local and regional commanders was not integrated into effective organisational structures at the national level, around which ordinary Afghan could rally. With no processes in place to reconcile these antagonisms or re-legitimate political power, the outcome could only be determined by political manipulation and battlefield combat. This set the scene for the second and third waves of the Afghanistan conflict.[156]

Pakistan's Efforts for Transfer of Power in Afghanistan

The strength army had achieved during Zia continuously thought of military solution over Afghan situation. Both General Mirza Aslam Beg and General Hamid Gul were loyal to Zia there for Pakistan military believed that after the Soviet exit the Islamists associated with Hekmatyar and other Pashtun groups would easily be able to topple the beleaguered Najibullah regime. But that didn't happen as the prediction of Pakistani charge d'affaires in Kabul, Fida Yunus came true. He predicted soon after Geneva Accords that the Najibullah Government would be resilient, arguing that the Mujahedeen groups were deeply divided, lacking cohesion and without a common political platform.[157]

On the eve of the completion of withdrawal, Soviet Foreign Minister Eduard Shevardnadze visited Islamabad to elicit Pakistan's cooperation in restraining a Mujahedeen assault in Kabul and encouraging transition to a government of reconciliation in Afghanistan. Shevardnadze's visit further pushed the Pakistan Government to put its efforts with Mujahedeen groups to form a representative body. The ISI managed to convene a shura or consultative council, at Madinatul Hujjaj near Rawalpindi with the participation of over four hundred Mujahedeen delegates, Afghan notables, and Ulema. On February 20, 1989, the Shura decided to nominate an Afghan Interim Government (AIG) and appointed Sibghatullah Mujahaddidi, as its President and Abdul Rab Rasul Sayyaf, as its Prime Minister. Gulbuddin Hekmatyar obtained the foreign affairs and Yunis Khalis was allocated the interior portfolio.[158] The AIG remained largely a façade on paper and dysfunctional as a representative entity, lacking the ability to devise a common policy or strategy to overturn and replace the Najibullah government in Kabul. In Afghanistan, major commanders, who were part of the different Mujahedeen groups, exercised influence and control in their respective areas, but rarely coordinated operations with each other. As time passed without any sign of Najibullah losing his grip over Kabul, the enthusiasm of the supporters of the AIG further dampened.

Some officials within the Pakistani ISI, who recognised the divisions within the AIG and the difficulty in uniting the Mujahedeen groups on a common platform, felt that Pakistan should recognise the AIG even if it was based on Pakistani soil. In their view, such recognition could become an incentive for cohesion within Mujahedeen groups. However, Foreign Office remained firm that AIG must be recognised only after it was able to establish inside Afghanistan. The ISI, with the help of Afghan Mujahedeen groups planned to capture the third largest city of Afghanistan, Jalalabad, and install AIG there. According to Steve Coll, Pakistan Prime Minister, Benazir Bhutto, gave the green light for the operation.[159] To the surprise of the over-optimistic Pakistani ISI, Afghan Army's 11 Division defeated the Mujahedeen at Jalalabad. The lack of coordination and air support to between various Mujahedeen doomed the Jalalabad offensive during April and June 1989. The Jalalabad operation bogged down in a costly siege, with high civilian casualties and an exodus of refugees from the city. The Jalalabad setback resulted in the removal of General Hamid Gul from the ISI. In the aftermath of Jalalabad operation, Najibullah gained confidence and gave up his apparent quest for power sharing with the Mujahedeen groups. Instead, Najibullah started portraying himself as an Afghan nationalist and the Mujahedeen groups as the agents of Pakistan. On the other hand, while Pakistan supported the idea of broad based government in Afghanistan, the hard-line groups in Mujahedeen and ISI insisted on exclusion of Najibullah from any negotiation process.

A power game among the main Mujahedeen groups had already ensued, with their sights fixed on Kabul. The tensions which were smoldering at the time of the Jalalabad campaign flared openly on July 9, 1989, in what came to be known as the Farkhar massacre.[160] Thirty commanders associated with Massoud's *shura-i-Nazar* including Dr Saed Husain, Commander Sr Malim Tariq, Commander Islamuddin, Commander Abdul Wadood, and Mawlawi Ezatullah were murdered by a commander from Hekmatyar's *Hizb-e-Islami* named Sayed Jamal. At the same time, Hekmatyar withdrew from the Interim Government in exile in Pakistan, claiming it needed to be elected if it was to be legitimate: ironic claim for someone aiming for exclusive power in Kabul.

In the mean time, United Nations also made some efforts to find out political solution of the Afghan problem. Benon Sevan, UN Envoy, met the Pakistan's new Prime Minister, Mian Nawaz Sharif, in late 1990.[161] Benon explained his ideas in full detail to Nawaz Sharif. His ideas focused on starting a direct or indirect dialogue between the Najibullah regime and the Mujahedeen groups for a broad based, if necessary interim, government in a power sharing arrangement. Gulbuddin Hekmatyar, Yunas Khalis, and Rasool Sayyaf, rejected any role for the United Nations. Rabbani's Jamait-i-Islami was ambivalent towards the UN while as the Afghan National Liberation front of Sibghatullah Mojaddedi, National Islamic Front of Sayed Ahmad Gailani, and Harkat-e-Enqilab-e-Islami Afghanistan of Maulvi Muhammad Nabi Mhammad were supportive of the idea.[162]

After Najibullah's Defence Minister, Shahnawaz Tanai defection, the attitude of the Kabul regime softened. In these circumstances, in May 1991, UN Secretary General Perez de Cuellar proposed a plan that envisaged a cease-fire between the Mujahedeen and Kabul regime forces, a cessation of arms supply by all countries involved in the conflict, and consultations for elections that would allow the Afghans to choose their own government. Najibullah showing his willingness to accept the proposal and cease-fire offer. Abdur Rab Rasool Sayyaf speaking on behalf of the AIG and Hekmatyar rejected the plan. Later on, AIG President Mujaddedi, declared that there could be no cease-fire with Najibullah.[163]

In early 1991, Iran proposed to cooperate with Pakistan to build a Mujahedeen united front and suggested a joint meeting of Pakistan, Iran and all major Mujahedeen groups. The first tri lateral meeting involving the three sides was organised in Islamabad in July 1991. The leaders of the seven Mujahedeen groups were joined in Islamabad by two additional Shia parties, Hizb-e-Wahdat led by Karim Khalili and Haji Muhammad Mohaqeq, and Harkat-e-Islami, headed by Sheikh Asif Mohsini. The follow up meeting in Tehran in September 1991 started on a discordant note and came to its logical end in a stalemate. Basically the absence of any clear parameters for cooperation killed the tri-lateral initiatives.

The main reason Pakistan's multidirectional efforts in 1990 and 1991 remained fruitless was that by this time the Mujahedeen leaders and commanders had become aware of the weakness of the Najibullah regime. It was the start of the end game for the seizure of Kabul. The influential commanders would not cooperate with each other or engage in major joint operations, fearing that such action could allow advantage to someone else.

Peshawar Accord

By the end of 1991, due to domestic pressures, Moscow

opened channels with various Afghans Islamist groups. Burhanuddin Rabbani, the Foreign Minister of the Afghan Interim Government visited Moscow in November.[164] However, Rabbani's visit turned out to be merely symbolic gesture as on December 25, 1991, the Soviet state disintegrated. The Soviet Union's collapse had left behind a power vacuum in Central Asia and Afghanistan which resulted in struggle for influence by regional and extra-regional powers.

Early 1992 presented a different scenario. The struggle for power among the Mujahedeen groups, in particular between Gulbuddin Hekmatyar and Ahmad Shah Masood, had begun. Each was trying to inveigle and win over Najibullah military generals to his side. On March 18, 1992, Najibullah announced the transfer of power to an interim government proposed by the UN. However the power struggle within the Najibullah party (Watan Party) accelerated the regime's collapse.

In the third week of March 1992, Benon Sevan wanted to meet Prime Minsiter Nawaz Sharif urgently. Sensing the changing scenario, the meeting was arranged for March 20 in Lahore, where Nawaz Sharif was joined by the newly appointed ISI chief, Lt. Gen. Javed Nasir. Benon Sevan issued a dramatic salvo, suggesting that Pakistan ask the Mujahedeen leaders to come up with an agreed panel of neutral personalities, and he would arrange a transfer of power to the panel in Kabul. In the meantime on April 16, 1992, President Najibullah resigned "more suddenly and less bloodily than most people had foreseen."[165] Nawaz immediately instructed the ISI chief to press the Mujahedeen groups to agree on a panel and coordinate the transfer of power. More than two weeks later, there was still no agreement on a panel of names, despite all the pressures that ISI could bring to bear on the Mujahedeen groups.

Different meetings were held between different Mujahedeen groups to finalise the names of the panel. Finally the breakthrough came on April 24, when ISI chief conveyed to the Prime Minister that an accord had been reached and was to be signed in Peshawar that evening. Witnessed by the Prime Minister and the Iranian foreign minister, who had flown to Peshawar from Tehran for that purpose, the leaders of the eight Afghan parties and the second in command from the Hizb Islami[166] placed their signature on what came to be known as the Peshawar Accord.[167]

In accordance with the Peshawar Accord, Sibghatullah Mujaddidi will head the Interim government for two months followed by Burhanuddin Rabbani for next four months. After the conclusion of the Rabbani's period, a Shura was to decide on the creation of a political system that would remain for two years, after which elections are scheduled to be held. Prime Ministership went to Hekmatyar's Hizb Islami and Ahmad Shah Masood got the post of Defence Minister. Deputy prime ministership was given to three parties, those of Yunas Khalis, Sayed Gailani, and Shia party Ittihad-e-Islami. Finally on April 24, 1992 Ahmad Shah Masood moved into Kabul and on April 28, 1992 Mujaddidi proceeded to Kabul in a big caravan and take over as President.

Fragmentation of Afghanistan and Islamabad's Concerns

The installation of Sibghatullah Mujaddidi as the President of the Interim Afghan Islamic Government apparently signaled the conclusion of the resistance's struggle against the Najibullah regime but it did not herald the end of the Afghan crisis. After the passage of close to two months following the April ceremonies inaugurating the new government, signs appeared of Mujaddidi's intention to extend his tenure.[168] But after the narrow escape from the missile attack on his plane, Mujaddidi passed on the presidency, as stipulated by the Peshawar Accord to 53 years old Burhanuddin Rabbani. In his farewell address, Mujaddidi called on Afghanistan's squabbling factions to try to heal the wounds from the struggle against a succession of Soviet installed regimes.[169]

On assumption of Power, Rabbani's immediate concern was a relentless strife between the forces of Hekmatyar and Masood around Kabul. The rest of Afghanistan was also divided up among power warlords, each with his own militia, generating revenue through taxes and road tolls. Jallaluddin Haqqani controlled Khost, Paktika and Paktia regions, Ismael Khan was entrenched in Herat; Abdul Rashid Dostum in Mazae-e-Sharif. Karim Khalil, Abdul Ali Mazari, and Sheikh Mohsini in the Hazarajat; and Haji Qadeer, Abdul Haq, and Deen Muhammad had influenced in the Jalalabad area. North of Jalalabad was Hekmatyar's territory. The only region of significance not under powerful warlord was Qandahar. [170]

Burhanuddin Rabbani began his extended tenure amid grave apprehensions whether the Shura would be convened. He agreed that he would surrender his power only if the Shura agreed to successor. He also insisted that his government would hold the Shura as promised to elect his successor. On December 29, 1992, 1335 Shura members from Afghanistan's 29 provinces, religious scholars, tribal leaders and rebel commanders met and began their deliberations in Kabul amidst tight security measures.[171] President Burhanuddin Rabbani was re-elected as a President of the transitional government for a period of two years. With the convening of the Shura, it could be said that the Peshawar Accord came to the logical end of its limited course.

Islamabad Accord

As the fighting continued in Afghanistan between different groups, Pakistan intervened again, Burhanuddin Rabbani and Gulbuddin Hekmatyar were invited by Prime Minister Nawaz Sharif to Islamabad.[172] An agreement was reached for sharing power on March 7, 1993 and it was agreed that Rabbani will continue as President and Hekmatyar was appointed Prime Minister. The new arrangement was to last until July 1994. It was also agreed that elections for president and parliament will be conducted. It was also agreed to create police and army force. But peace remained elusive. Hekmatyar, now Prime Minister, was unwilling to enter Kabul without his forces or the exit of Panjshiris and other pro-Ahmad Shah Masood forces. According to Islamabad Accord, the prime minister and president were to decide the cabinet in consultation with each other and other Mujahedeen leaders. Hekmatyar's objection to Masood keeping the portfolio of defence minister became a point of contention and resulted in early breakdown of the Islamabad Accord.[173]

Afghanistan's misfortune thus persisted, as none of the Mujahedeen leaders was capable of inspiring confidence among his peers and building viable alliance that could steer the country towards calm and normalcy. Of the two major military leaders, Ahmad Shah Masood and Gulbuddin Hekmatyar, the former was better disposed to reaching out to others, yet he remained essentially insular, suspicious, and parochial. Dostum, Ismael Khan, Jallaluddin Haqqani, and other prominent commanders remained on the periphery, preoccupied with their regional holds. High profile political leaders inclined to build and work within coalition, in particular Rabbani, Majaddidi, and Gilani, lacked military muscle or the backing of strong commanders. Afghanistan remained divided, mired in conflict and ungoverned. The Mujahedeen's failure to accommodate each other and work together within an agreed political framework revealed fundamentalist and radical Islam's inability to provide functional national governance.[174]

Pakistan-Afghanistan after Soviet Union Withdrawal

Afghanistan was in a state of virtual disintegration at the end of 1994.[175] The situation was worsened day by day as the fighting continued between the different Mujahedeen groups. In these circumstances, the people of Afghanistan saw a new hope in the form of a new unexpected force, the Taliban. The emergence of Taliban was grounded in many factors; cold war rivalries, Soviet Union intervention in Afghanistan, revolution in Iran, and the most important factor was US after fall of Soviet Union left Afghanistan destabilised and destroyed.

By the mid 1990's, discontent was on the rise throughout the country, but Qandahar and Helmand regions were suffering the most, as these areas were not under the control of a major warlord who could maintain any semblance of order. Over a dozen low ranking local commanders' affiliated with various parties operated in this region, who plundered the population at will. The situation was so bad, that from Chaman on the Pakistani side of the border to Qandhar, a distance of barely 120 kilometers, local commanders erected more than twenty toll-posts to extort money to allow passage of trading goods.[176] According to Ahmed Rashid, the warlords sold off everything of Qandhar to Pakistani traders to make money, stripping down telephone wires and poles, cutting trees, selling off factories, machinery and even road rollers to scrap merchants.[177] They seized homes and farms, threw out their occupants and handed them over to their supporters.[178] The Commanders abused the population at will, kidnapping young girls and boys for their sexual pleasure, robbing merchants in the bazaars and fighting and brawling in the streets.[179]

Pakistan's Surge for Strategic Depth

The protracted internecine conflict in Afghanistan 1992-1995, the increasingly assertive and pro-Iranian stance of the Rabbani administration and Hekmatyar's inability to gain control of Kabul had put serious constraints for Pakistan's policy in Afghanistan. The leadership in Pakistan witnessed difficulties to realise its aim to access to Central Asia and securing its much acclaimed 'strategic depth' against India. Pakistan's two decades long involvement in Afghanistan had led to the perception within the Pakistani military elite that given the sacrifices made by Pakistan on behalf of the Afghans, during their fighting against the Soviets, Islamabad had the right to have a friendly[180], subservient regime in Kabul.[181] In this connection, Pakistan saw a ray of hope in the form of Taliban to fulfil its interests.[182] The Taliban's rapid success between 1995 and 1996 emboldened Islamabad to support the militia totally as it visualised that through this irregular armed formation it could finally eliminate what it saw as the anti-Pakistan 'Northern Alliance'.[183] As a matter of fact, the military elite's commitment to support the Taliban had become firmer after the Taliban's capture of Herat in September 1995 and the subsequent attack on Pakistan's embassy in Kabul by an enraged Afghan mob which blamed Islamabad for the attack on Herat.[184]

According to Rasul Rais, due to the wide gulf between Taliban and Iran on theological matters, it was natural for the Taliban to look towards Pakistan for whatever assistance it needed. On the other side, Pakistan, under the compulsive security environment of the region, needed the Taliban on its side to influence its rivals in Afghanistan. Pakistan offered them intelligence support and strategic advice in their key battles, and helped them negotiate political deals with local commanders and warlords.[185]

However, the isolation of the Taliban and their grievances against the international community over non-recognition and the routinely harsh international criticism of the Taliban hardened Mullah Omar's view that only a military approach could bring success to the Taliban. He grew more dependent on the foreign militant elements, particularly the Arabs. Osama bin Laden[186] came to Kandahar in late 1996 started building relations with Taliban leadership and started providing financial help to the cash starved Taliban. The Al Qaeda influence on Omar became visible when, two years after the capture of the Hazarajat and one year after his decree to preserve the eighteen hundred old colossal Buddhas carved into the sandstone hills facing the city of Bamiyan, the statues were allowed to be defiled.[187]

United Nations and Taliban

After the advent of the Taliban, the UN Secretary General appointed three successive special representatives for Afghanistan: Mehmoud Mestiri from January 1995 to June 1996, Norbert Holl from July 1996 to November 1997, and James N'gobi from December 1997 to December 1998, all serving as head of the UN Special Mission in Afghanistan (UNSMA). The UN's efforts mostly revolved around encouraging cease-fires, preventing attacks against cities, forming commissions for reconciliation, and the more ambitious goals of promoting a broad based government and prohibiting the supply of arms to the warring factions.

United Nations representatives had some success in bringing the opposite parties together. In February 1997, Norbert Holl was able to organise working level talks between the Taliban, Hizb-e-Wahdat, and Rashid Dostum's Junbish-e-Milli to focus on the question of exchange of prisoners. In April-May 1998, the UN and the OIC launched a significant effort. They developed a proposal for the formation of a commission of Ulema to be nominated by the Taliban and the Northern Alliance that would decide measures for restoration of peace and stability in Afghanistan.[188] But these efforts resulted in disappointment.

United Nations also tried to reconciliate different factions in Afghanistan through its special envoy. In this case UN tried to bring outside players into confidence as well. The most significant of these initiatives was Lakhhdar Brahimi's "Six-plus-Two" format to get Afghanistan's six neighbours and Russia and the United States. Since its inception in early 1998, the arrangement became a forum for the eight participants, mostly at the ambassadorial level, to discuss the situation in Afghanistan. Although the group failed to pressure the contending Afghan factions for peace and reconciliation, but the group remained hostage to the interests of the individual members and their rivalries and differing interests. After the attacks on the US embassies in Kenya and Tanzania in August 1998, the US priority shifted to putting pressure on the Taliban to hand over Osama bin Laden, the leader of the Al Qaeda, who is believed to be behind the attacks. So at the behest of the United States, the United Nations now started to consider imposing sanctions against the Taliban for providing safe haven to Al Qaeda. The US view of the Taliban had now turned from ambivalence to hostility.

US Policy towards Taliban

Here our purpose is not to give a detailed account of U.S. Taliban policy, but to give a brief outlook of how the initial US ambivalence towards Taliban had turned to hostility. Initially US policy towards Taliban was friendly and they were comfortable with Taliban in Afghanistan due to two major reasons: first, to counter the Iranian influence in Afghanistan and secondly, they were looking for economic interests (oil and gas pipeline) in newly independent states of Central Asia through Afghanistan.[189] Union Oil Company of California, UNOCAL, was one of the first in the area as soon as the prospects of accesses to the energy resources of the Caspian Basin materialised with the breakup of Soviet Union. UNOCAL had its eyes on a possible project for a gas pipeline over 1500 kilometers long from Turkmenistan to Pakistan through Afghanistan, initially estimated at $2.5 billion. The company set up its office in Kandahar in 1996. Its rivalry with an Argentinean oil company, Bridas, for the same project raised considerable speculations about a new "great game" in the region and about funding of the Taliban by the two interested parties.[190]

In April 1998, US permanent representative to the UN, Bill Richardson along with Ambassador Thomas Simons and Assistant Secretary of State Karl Rick visited Kabul. This was the end of the informal contacts that United States had continued to maintain with Taliban. Richardson and others meet the Afghan President Mullah Rabbani and other Taliban officials for three hours. At that Taliban was looking for assistance to revive their economy and they were also looking for recognition and financial assistance to revive an economy in a state of total collapse. Mr Richardson discussed narcotics control and women's rights with the Taliban President. He said the Taliban had agreed to let women study at the university level and to work outside the home without being chaperoned by the male relative.[191] Raiz Muhammad Khan says that following the meeting, Mullah Rabbani had promised to open girl's schools, provided funds were made available, and to relax the ban on NGO operations. He further suggested that the United States and Saudi Arabia could bring a case in an Afghan court against Osama on the basis of evidence, and Taliban government would respect the verdict.[192] But according to Steve Coll, at that time Osama was a secondary issue for the Americans.[193]

But when Madeleine Albright became Secretary of State, she started bringing change in US policy regarding Taliban from being sympathetic to punitive. Albright visited Pakistan in November 1997 during her visit to Pakistan Albright had expressed her dislike of the Taliban regime because of their policies especially related to the violation of human rights, women rights, gender discrimination and Osama Bin Laden.

Americans pressurised Nawaz Sharif to influence the Taliban and publically condemn "terrorist training camps" in Afghanistan. Pakistan ISI Chief Khwaja Ziauddin visited Kandahar and requested the Taliban to close down terrorist training camps. UN Security Council resolution gave the Taliban until November 14, to handover Bin Laden or face sanction. US Under Secretary of State, Strobe Talbott, held a meeting with several Taliban representative in February, 1999, at Islamabad in order to motivate Mullah Omar to handover Bin Laden. The Afghan crises would enter a new phase by mid 1999. The domestic turmoil in Pakistan and the evolution of a clearer policy emerging from Washington, would lead to vigorous Pakistani attempts to bring about an easing of tensions between the US and Taliban. This was a stance that proved to be futile.[194]

United States was basically without understanding Taliban movement supporting them for strategic and economic reasons. They inappropriately perceived them as a strategic asset against Iran. But, 9/11 attacks on America brought a metamorphic change in US Taliban policy, resulted in US war against terrorism.

Military Regime in Pakistan and Afghanistan

On October 12, 1999, the Pakistan Army carried out its third bloodless coup in the country's then 52 years old chequered history by arresting the Prime Minister and declaring a state of emergency. The coup was ostensibly sparked by Sharif's orders to retire the incumbent Chief of the Army Staff and replace him with the then Director General of the ISI, Lieutenant General Ziauddin Butt, a Sharif loyalist. This motivated the Commander of the army's X Corps, Lt. General Mahmud Ahmad and Lt. General Muhammad Aziz to depose the Sharif regime and install General Musharraf as the 'Chief Executive' of Pakistan.[195]

After the takeover, General Musharraf portrayed his regime as reformist and determined to deal with the staggering political and economic problems faced by Pakistan. He promised wide-ranging internal reforms, but announced that there would be no change in the foreign policy. This meant that Pakistan would continue the traditional policy on Afghanistan and Kashmir. Therefore, the army of Pakistan continued the support of Taliban.

The Musharraf regime pressed on with bolstering the Taliban even with the intensifying US apprehensions about the presence of Osama Bin Laden in Kandahar. Between May and October 2000, Pakistan escalated its assistance to the Taliban in a bid to expand the militia's operational reach to Ahmed Shah Masood's stronghold centred at Taloqan in northeastern Afghanistan. The Taliban, helped by Pakistani piloted aircraft and regular troops in civilian attire, were successfully in seizing Taloqan in June 2000. In 2001, US continued its pressure on Pakistan over the presence of Osama Bin Laden in Afghanistan, but Pakistan continued its delaying tactics. However, on September 11, 2001 the massive terrorist attacks on the Pentagon and the Twin Towers in New York, purportedly carried out by elements of Al Qaeda essentially dealt a deathblow to the Pakistani stratagem vis-à-vis Afghanistan.

Pakistan's military establishments generally argue that once Taliban settled down and established control over the entirety of Afghanistan, they would be ripe to undergo an internal metamorphosis towards moderation. This was an illusion, if not a pretext, to defend a regime that seemed friendly and completely dependent on Pakistan. No doubt, the Taliban enjoyed certain grass-root support and legitimacy and were able to bring peace and successfully reintegrate much of Afghanistan. But most of the world saw them as an abomination. Due to pro-Taliban policy, Pakistan lost much of the goodwill it had earned over a decade among most Afghans, in addition to the Afghan Mujahedeen leadership and significant elements within the Afghan elite.[196]

Indo-Afghan relations saw many ups and downs over the course of their history. Both India and Afghanistan have the disputes with Pakistan, which provides them a common adversary Pakistan. The Pashtun issues between Afghanistan and India, and Kashmir Issue between India and Pakistan have brought India and Afghanistan closer to cooperate on strategic front as both nations face the insurgencies supported and harboured by Pakistan. India's cordial relations with Afghanistan began with Zahir Shah. Pakistan perceived that India used its engagement with Afghanistan to exaggerate Afghan-Pakistan dispute. India fears that the use of Afghan soil against India in case of war will help incursion in Kashmir.

However, the Afghans still feel that India's role play during the period of Soviet invasion was betrayal to the traditional relations of both countries. A change as expected occurred in their relations during the Mujahideen period when India became a distant neighbour. It was only during 1990s when civil war broke out India came to support Tajik faction viewed as prone to be more secular than other. It is to be noted that India continuously supported Northern Alliance by supplying arms, aid and intelligence when Taliban took over whole Afghanistan in mid 1990s.

The post-Taliban period was almost in favour of India. By the time, however, Afghanistan was ravaged by American war. Therefore, investment for rebuilding the nation has become very important and the end the proxy war was put in front line of crisis management by being close to the neighbouring countries. India as a growing economy and a democratic nation having good public and political space in Afghanistan was prepared by Afghanistan as main actor in the nation building process. Accordingly, India has played for mutual economic benefits and for bringing in good supply line for its growing economy fostering peace and prosperity for entire region.

References

1. Ahmed Rashid, *The Taliban* (London: Yale University Press, 2001), 07.
2. *www.tribalanalysiscenter.com*
3. Ian Stephon, *Horned Moon* (London: Wrnest Benn, 1963), 108 cited by Mohibullah Durani and Ashraf Khan, "Pakistan-Afghanistan Relations: Historical Mirror", *The Dialogue* Vol. 4, no. 1, (Peshawar: Jan-March 2009), 25. See also Aparna Pande, *Explaining Pakistan's Foreign Policy: Escaping India,* (Oxon: Rout- ledge Contemporary South Asia, 2011), 81.
4. A.Z. Hilali, "The Soviet Penetration into Afghanistan and the Marxist Coup," *The Journal of Salavic Military Studies,* Vol. 18, issue, 04, January 12, 2005, pp. 673-716.
5. *Ibid.*
6. *Ibid.*
7. Rahul Roy Chaudhury, "Pakistan", in *Afghanistan: To 2015 and Beyond,* ed. Toby Dodge and Nicholas Redman (Routledge: 2012), 167.

8. *Ibid*, 167.
9. Rasul Bakhsh Rais, "Afghanistan and Pakistan: Difficult Neighbours", *NBR Analysis,* Vol. 19, No. 5, (Washington DC: December 2008), p. 15.
10. Rizwan Hussain, *Pakistan and the Emergence of Islamic Militancy in Afghanistan* (Hampshire: Ashgate Publishing Ltd., 2005), 16.
11. *Ibid.*, p. 21.
12. *Ibid,* p. 44,
13. Official Records of the UN General Assembly Plenary Meeting, Ninety-Second Plenary Meeting , September 30, 1947, "Admission of Pakistan and Yemen to Membership in the United Nations," Document A/399, p. 314.
14. Bijan Omrani, "The Durand Line: History and Problems of the Afghan –Pakistan Border," *Asian Affairs,* Vol. XL, No. 11, (London: July 2009), pp. 177-195.
15. Daveed Garttenstein-Ross and Tara Vassefi, "The Forgotten History of Afghanistan-Pakistan Relations," *Yale Journal of International Affairs*, March 2012, p. 40 *http://yalejournal.org/wp-content/uploads/2012/04/Article-Gartenstein_Ross-and-Vassefi.pdf*
16. *Ibid*, p. 40.
17. *Ibid*, p. 41 see also James W. Spain, "Pakistan's North West Frontier," *Middle East Journal,* Vol. 8, No. 1, (Washington DC: Winter 1954), 27-40.
18. The tribes are Baluchis, Ketranis, Nuristanis, Brahui, Munjis, Chitralis, Shinas, Gujaris, Hazaras, Kowars, Savis, Tajiks, Hindkos, Dameli, Kalamis, Urmurs, Wakhis, Gawar_batis, Badeshi, Khirgiz, Burushos, etc.

    Erinn Banting, *Afghanistan the People* (New York: Crabtree Publishing Company, 2003), 14.
19. K P Misra, *Afghanistan in Crises* (New Delhi: Vikas Publishing House, 1981), 87.
20. Rizwan Hussain, 64-65.
21. Dilip Mukerjee, "Afghanistan under Daud: Relations with Neighbouring State", *Asian Survey,* Vol. 15, No. 4, (California: April 1975), pp. 301-12.
22. Kabulian.net, *http://www.angelfire.com/ak5/farda/Calendar.html* accessed on 30/01/2013.
23. Ziba Moshaver, *Nuclear Weapons Proliferation in the Indian Subcontinent,* (New York: St. Martin's Press, 1991), p. 4-7.
24. 'The Dictionary,' Macmillan Dictionary of British and European History Since 1914, 1919.

25. *www.news.uniquepakistan.com.pk*
26. "Discussion with Afghanistan Concerning Afghan Requests for Financial Assistance and Provision of Military Equipments; Elevation of the American Legation in Afghanistan to the Status of Embassy," *Foreign Relations of the United States (FRUS)*, Vol. 5, Part 1, (U.S Government Printing Press, 1948), 488.
27. Angelo Rasanayagam, *Afghanistan: A Modern History* (London and New York: I. B. Tauris, 2002), 28.
28. Uzbekistan Area Handbook Series, *Afghanistan: A Country Study*, (Baton Rouge: Claitor's Publishing Division, 2001), 58.
29. Considering of Basic United States Security Interests in the Near East and South Asia, *FRUS*, Vol. 6, (US Government Printing Press Office, 1949), 07.
30. Rizwan Hussain, 68.
31. Rasanayagam, 27.
32. The other members are Thailand, Philippines, Australia, New Zealand, France, Great Britain and USA.
33. The other members are Iraq, Iran, Turkey and Great Britain.
34. Jean-Luc Racine, "Pakistan in the Great Game", in *A History of Pakistan and its Origins*, ed. Christophe Jaffrelot (London: Anthem Press, 2002), 100.
35. Amin Saikal, *Modern Afghanistan: A History of Struggle and Survival* (New York: I. B. Tauris, 2004), 122.
36. Hussain, 71.
37. Kalim Bahadur, "Pakistan's Policy Towards Afghanistan" in *Afghanistan in Crises*, ed. K P Mishra (New Delhi: Vikas Publishing House, 1981), pp. 84-100.
38. *Ibid*, pp. 84-100.
39. *www.digitalarchive.wilsoncenter.org*
40. Rasanayagam, 33.
41. Kalim Bahadur, 91, (84-100).
42. "Memorandum of Conversation between the Afghan Ambassador (Maiwandwal) and the Assistant Secretary of State for Near Eastern and South Asian Affairs (Rountree), Department of State," *FRUS*, Vol. XV, (Washington, October 13, 1958), p. 241. *www.mea.gov.in*
43. M. Hussain Karkar, *Afghanistan: The Soviet invasion and the Afghan Response, 1979-1982* (Berkeley: California University Press, 1995), 09.
44. Feisal Khan, "Why Borrow Trouble for yourself and Lend it to Neighbors? Understanding the Historical Roots of Pakistan

Afghan Policy," *Asian Affairs An American Review*, Vol. 37, issue. 04, October 2010, pp. 171-189.

45. Feisal Khan, 171-189.
46. Telegram from the Department of State to the Embassy in Afghanistan, *FRUS*, 1961-63, Vol. XIX, South Asia, 347.
47. Rizwan Hussain, p. 73.
48. For details about 1964 Constitution see, L. Dupree, *Afghanistan* (Princeton: Princeton University Press, 1973).
49. www,Khyber.org
50. Rifaat Hussain, "Pakistan's Relations with Afghanistan: Continuity and Change", *www.docstoc.com/docs/24097140/pakistan-s-relations-with-afghanistan-continuity-and-change* accessed on 06/02/2013.
51. *www.qurtuba.edu.pk*
52. Mujtaba Razvi, *The Frontiers of Pakistan: A Study of Frontier Problems in Pakistan's Foreign Policy* (Karachi: National Publishing House, 1971), 159-63.
53. Dr Noor Shah, *Pak-Afghan Relations: In the Perspective of War on Terrorism, http://eprints.hec.gov.pk/4293/* , accessed on 07/02/2013.
54. Anatol Lieven, *Pakistan: A Hard Country,* (London: Penguin Books, 2011), 59.
55. Kalim Bahadur, "Pakistan Foreign Policy Towards Afghanistan," *International Studies*, January 01, 1980.
56. *Ibid.*
57. Tehseena Usman, "Trust Deficit in Pak-Afghan Relations and its Implications: A Historical Perspective (19478-2001)," *Dialogue,* (1819-6462), 2013, pp. 311 (303-326).
58. Kalim Bahadur, Pakistan's policy.
59. Arney George, *Afghanistan,* (London: Mandarin Paperbacks, 1990), p. 65, cited in Angelo Rasanayagam, *Afghanistan: A Modern History,* p. 74.
60. Peoples Democratic Party of Afghanistan (PDPA) was a political Party established on January 1, 1965 by Nur Mohammad Taraki and Babrak Karmal. Due to ideological and economic differences party broke down into several political sects. The two main were Khalqs led by Taraki and Parchams led by Karmal.
61. Shaista Wahab and Barry Youngerman, *A Brief History of Afghanistan* (New York: Infobase Publishing, 2007), p. 129.
62. Rasanayagam, p. 61.
63. Dilip Mukerjee, p. 303.

64. Marvin G Weinbaum, *Pakistan and Afghanistan: Resistance and Reconstruction,* (San Francisco: Westview Press, 1994), p. 04.
65. Hussain, 78.
66. Marvin G Weinbaum, *Pakistan and Afghanistan: Resistance and Reconstruction* (San Francisco: Westview Press, 1994), p. 05.
67. Kalim Bahadur, Pakistan's Policy.
68. General Naseerullah Babur interview to A H Amin in March 2001, and published in a monthly *Defence Journal* (Rawalpindi: April 2001). See also Edward Girarde, *Afghanistan: the Soviet War* (Oxen: Routledge Publishers, 2011), 166.
69. Anees Jillani, "Pak Afghan Relations: 1958 to 1988", *Pakistan Horizon,* Vol. 46, No. 1, (Karachi: January 1993), pp. 35-45.
70. Ahmad Rashir Malik, "Warming Ties with Russia", *Oriental Review, http://orientalreview.org/2011/05/25/warming-ties-with-russia/* accessed on 14/02/3013.
71. Selig S. Harrison, *In Afghanistan's Shadow: Balouch Nationalism and Soviet Temptation,* (New York: Carnegie Endowment for International Peace, 1981), 129.
72. Jagmohan Meher, "United States and Afghanistan: A Historical Perspective", in *South Asia Today,* ed. Goal Singh and Ramesh Chauhan (New Delhi: Anamika Publishers, 2005), 231.
73. Kalim Bahadur, Pakistan's policy.
74. *Ibid.*
75. Mohammad Yahya. Akhter, "Electoral Politics and Corruption Under Civilian Rule in Post- 1971 Pakistan," *South Asian Survey,* Vol. 11, Issue 01, January 03, 200, pp. 75-93.
76. Nine parties are: Tehrik-i-istalal (TI), Jamaat-i-Islami (JI), Jamaat-ulama-i-islam (JUI), Jamaat-i-ulma-i-Pakistan (JUP), Pakistan Muslim League- Pagaro (PLL(P)), National Democratic Party (NDP), Pakistan Democratic Party (PDP), Khaksat Tehrik (KT) and Azad Kashmir Muslim Conference (AKMC).
77. Iftikhar H. Malik, *The History of Pakistan* (London: Greenwood Press, 2008), 168.
78. Ian Talbot, *Pakistan: A modern History* (London: Hurst and company, 1998), 240.
79. Abdul Samad Ghaus, *The Fall of Afghanistan: An Insider's Account* (London: Brassey's International Defence Publishers, 1988), 141.
80. President Mohammad Daoud's speech at Lahore in *Foreign Affairs – Pakistan,* Islamabad: Ministry of Foreign Affairs, Vol. VI, issue 3, March 1978. Quoted in Rizwan Hussain, *Pakistan and the Emergence of Islamic Militancy in Afghanistan,* 94.

81. Wahab and Youngerman, 134.
82. A. Z. Hilali, "The Soviet Penetration into Afghanistan and the Marxist Coup", *The Journal of Slavic Military Studies*, Vol. 18, No. 4 (London), p. 709.
83. *Ibid,* p. 709.
84. SAVAK i.e. *Sazeman-e Ettelaat va Amniyat-e Keshvar* (Organisation of Intelligence and National Security) was a secret police, domestic security and intelligence service established by Iran's Mohammad Reza Shah and operated from 1957 to 1979.
85. A. Z. Hilali, "The Soviet Penetration into Afghanistan and the Marxist Coup", p. 710.
86. *Ibid,* pp. 709-710.
87. *Ibid,* pp. 709-710.
88. Mike Barry, *The Afghan Resistance from the Great Mongol till the Soviet Invasion* (Paris: Flammarion Publications, 1989), 314.
89. Z. Hilali, "The Soviet Penetration into Afghanistan and the Marxist Coup, p. 710.
90. M.S. Agwani, "The Saur Revolution and After," *International Studies*, Vol. 19, No. 04 January 01, 1980, pp. 557-573.
91. A. Z. Hilali, The Soviet Penetration into Afghanistan and the Marxist Coup, pp. 710-11.
92. *Saur* is a Persian word meaning April, the month in Afghan calendar when the revolution took place.
93. M.S. Agwani, "The *Saur* Revolution and After", p. 212.
94. M.S. Agwani, "The *Saur* Revolution and After", in *Afghanistan in Crisis,* ed. K P Mishra, (New Delhi: Vikas Publishing House, 1981), pp. 01-17.
95. Hussain, pp. 95-96.
96. *Ibid,* p. 96.
97. Jillani, p. 41.
98. Gen. Khalid Mahmud Arif, *Working with Zia: Pakistan's Power Politics, 1977-1988* (Karachi: Oxford University Press, 1995), 307, quoted in Hussain Haqqani, *Pakistan Between Mosque and Military* (Washington DC: Carnegie Endowment for International Peace, 2005), p. 176. All subsequent references to the Zia-ul-Haq – Taraki conversation are from this source.
99. Hussain, p. 98.
100. John C. Griffiths, *Afghanistan: Land of Conflict and Beauty* (London: Andre Deutsch, 2011), p. 173.
101. Hussain, p. 98.

102. Stephen Tanner, *Afghanistan: A Military History from Alexander the Great to the Fall of Taliban* (USA: Da Capo Press, 2003), pp. 231-32.
103. Rasanayagam, p. 79.
104. Hafez Malik, "Dilemmas of National Security and Cooperation," in *Dilemmas of National Security and Cooperation in India and Pakistan*, ed. Hafeez Malik, (London: Macmillan Press Ltd., 1993), pp. 01-33.
105. Robert G. Wirsing, *Pakistan's Security Under Zia 1977-1988*, (New York: St. Martine's, 1991), p. 79.
106. *Ibid,* p. 79.
107. *Ibid,* p. 79.
108. *Ibid,* p.79.
109. Hussain, pp. 104-06.
110. In NWFP the bases were located in Bannu, Batgram, Chitral, Chrat, Dir, Dera Adam Khalil, Hangu, Kohat, Mardan, Mastung, Miranshah, Nowshera, Pabi. Parachinar, Warsak and Wazistan.
111. In Baluchistan, the bases were in Chagai, Zhob, Nushki, Pishin, Sibi and Quetta.
112. In Punjab the bases were located in Esa Khel, Guranwala Cantt, Okara Cantt, Attock, Jhelum Cantt, Kharian Cantt and Mianwali Kalabagh.
113. A.Z. Hilali, *US – Pakistan Relationship: Soviet Invasion of Afghanistan* (Hants: Ashgate Publishing Limited, 2005), p. 122.
114. *www.publications.parliament.uk*
115. M.S. Agwani, p. 10.
116. Hussain, pp. 111.
117. Rasanayagam, p. 82.
118. In February 1979, US Ambassador Adolph Dubs was kidnapped by radical Afghan group, *Sitm-e-Melli.* Against American advice, Afghan rescue team launched operation ended up killing the kidnappers and the Ambassador. By this incident US had ended his aid programmes and reduced Diplomatic profile.
119. Wahab and Youngerman, p. 152.
120. A.Z. Hilali, "The Soviet Penetration into Afghanistan and the Marxist Coup, p. 715.
121. Wahab and Youngerman, p. 155.
122. A.Z. Hilali, "The Soviet Penetration into Afghanistan and the Marxist Coup, p. 715.
123. Wahab and Youngerman, p. 157.

124. Darrel J. Bennett, Jr, "From the Carter to the Bush Doctrine: An In-Depth Analysis of US Middle Eastern Policy", Policy Analysis Paper, Centre for the Study of the Presidency and Congress (Washington: 2007), www.thepresidency.org/storage/documents/Calkins/Bennett.pdf , cited on 27-02-2013 at 10 PM.
125. Hussain, p. 114.
126. Haqqani, p. 186.
127. Raiz M Khan, p. 25.
128. Haqqani, p. 188.
129. Hussain, p. 119.
130. *Ibid,* p. 120.
131. Wahab and Youngerman, p. 172.
132. Khan, p. 72.
133. Khan, p. 79.
134. *Ibid,* p. 80.
135. Racine, p.107.
136. Selig S. Harrison quoted in *Jihad Groups, Nuclear Pakistan and the New Great Game,* ed. M. Ahsan Ahrari (Carlisle, PA: Strategic Studies Institute, US Army War College, August 2001), p. 04.
137. Selig S. Harrison, "Inside the Afghan Talks", *Foreign Policy,* No. 72, (Washington: Autumn 1988), pp. 31-60.
138. Hussain Haqqani, "Breaking Up is Not Hard to Do", *Foreign Affairs*, Vol. 92, No. 2, (New York: March-April 2013), pp. 64-76.
139. A.Z. Hilali, "The Costs and Benefits of the Afghan War for Pakistan", *Contemporary South Asia,* Vol. 11, No. 3, (2002), pp. 291-310.
140. Hussain, p. 123.
141. Robert Wirsing, Pakistan's Security Under Zia 1977-1988, p. 65.
142. Harrison, p. 36.
143. *www.dtic.mil.*
144. *Ibid,* pp. 36-37.
145. Khan, p. 92.
146. Harrison, p. 44.
147. *Ibid,* p. 46.
148. *Ibid,* p. 49.
149. *www.academon.com*
150. *Nation* (Lahore), November 16, 1987.
151. Khan, p. 233.
152. Diego Cordovez and Selig S. Harrison, *Out of Afghanistan: The Inside story of the Soviet Withdrawal,* (New York : Oxford University Press, 1995), p. 368.

153. Anatoly S. Chernyaev, *My Six Years with Gorbachev* (University Park: The Pennsylvania State University Press, 2000). p. 161.
154. William Maley, *The Afghanistan Wars* (Hampshire: Palgrave Macmillan, 2002), p. 145.
155. Barnett R. Rubin, "Soviet Lessons of Afghanistan Assure Pullout Will Go On", *Los Angeles Times,* November 14, 1988.
156. *Ibid,* p. 152.
157. Raiz Mohammad Khan, *Afghanistan and Pakistan: Conflict, Extremism, and Resistance to Modernity* (New Delhi: Oxford University Press, 2011), p. 17.
158. After nominating Mujahaddidi and Sayyaf as President and Prime Minister of AIG respectively, the bitterness between the hard line and moderate groups was so strong that it prevented approval of either of the two personalities to the top position resulted into appointment of Muhammad Nabi Muhammadi as President and Engineer Ahmed Shah as Prime Minister.
159. Steve Coll, *Ghost Wars* (New York: Penguin Books, 2004) p. 193.
160. Rob Johnson, *A Region in Turmoil: South Asian Conflicts Since 1947* (London: Reaktion Books, 2005), p. 184.
161. Pakistan President Ghulam Ishaq Khan dismissed the Benazir Government in August 1990, and the subsequent elections brought about a new coalition led by Nawaz Sharif.
162. Raiz Mohammad Khan, *Afghanistan and Pakistan: Conflict, Extremism, and Resistance to Modernity*, p. 24.
163. *Ibid,* p. 25.
164. Burhanuddin Rabbani became the Foreign Minister of AIG after the resignation of Hekmatyar in August 1989.
165. The Afghans Nervous End Game, *The Economist* (US), April 25, 1992.
166. As Gulbuddin Hekmatyar refused to attend the meeting, as he remained on the outskirts of Kabul, confronting his rival Ahmad Shah Masood.
167. Raiz Mohammad Khan, *Afghanistan and Pakistan: Conflict, Extremism, and Resistance to Modernity*, p. 45.
168. Afghanistan President Warns of a Conspiracy Against Him, *The New York Times,* June 1, 1992.
169. For Once, Afghanistan Sees a Peaceful Transition, *The New York Times,* June 29, 1992.
170. Raiz Mohammad Khan, *Afghanistan and Pakistan: Conflict, Extremism, and Resistance to Modernity*, p. 49.
171. Afghans Picking Chief Under Rebel Threat, *The New York Times,* December 30, 1992.

172. Afghans Appear Closer to Peace, *The New York Times,* March 4, 1993.
173. Raiz Mohammad Khan, *Afghanistan and Pakistan: Conflict, Extremism, and Resistance to Modernity*, p. 50.
174. *Ibid,* p. 54.
175. Taliban- Part 1- Overview and Background," APS Diplomat Redrawing the Islamic Map, September 10, 2001.
176. *Ibid,* p. 57.
177. *www.search.barnesandnoble.com*
178. *Ibid.*
179. Ahmed Rashid, *Taliban: The Story of the Afghan Warlords* (London, Pan Books: 2001), p. 21.
180. 'Steering Our Own Path," *Indian Express*, October 07, 2009.
181. Hussain, p. 202.
182. www.cia.gov
183. Ahmad Shah Masoud and Abdul Rashid Dostum, created the United Front (Northern Alliance) against the Taliban. Later Masoud forged alliance with several Pushtun, Uzbek and Hazara factions.
184. Kamal Matinuddin, *The Taliban Phenomenon: Afghanistan 1994-1997* (London: Oxford University Press, 2000), p. 24.
185. Rasul Bakhsh Rais, *Recovering the Frontier State: War, Ethnicity and State in Afghanistan* (Plymouth, UK: Lexington Books, 2008) p. 70.
186. Osama Bin Laden, a member of the Saudi billionaire Bin Laden family, came to Peshawar during 1980's to help Afghan Jihad against Soviets. After establishing Al-Qaeda, he moved to Sudan in 1992, where he was hounded by U.S. intelligence, forcing him to return to Afghanistan in May 1996.
187. Khan, *Afghanistan and Pakistan: Conflict, Extremism, and Resistance to Modernity,* p. 80.
188. *Ibid,* p. 72.
189. *Ibid,* p. 75.
190. For full details see, Ahmed Rashid, *Taliban: The Story of the Afghan Warlords*, pp. 157-182.
191. Afghanistan Factions Agree to Cease-Fire, *New York Times,* April 18, 1998. See also www.americanprowler
192. Khan, *Afghanistan and Pakistan: Conflict, Extremism, and Resistance to Modernity,* p. 76.
193. Steve Coll, *Ghost Wars*, p. 384.
194. Hussain, p. 218.
195. *Ibid,* p. 220.
196. *Ibid,* p. 85.

Chapter – III

Anglo-Russian Imperialism: Durand Line and Pakhtoonistan

Russia from time of Peter the Great (1622-1725) always has strived to have access to warm water port in Indian Ocean[1] and it was due to that aim that the confronted Russia with British imperialism in Central Asia and the Indian sub-continent. The issue also resulted in confrontation of both great powers for gaining position over Afghanistan. Afghanistan is a contemporary independent country, when the Afghan tribes through a Jirga of elders selected Ahmad Shah Abadali as the King which before there was no such thing as Afghanistan. He is said to be the first that took the initiative of bringing and uniting all Afghan districts into one political identity of Afghanistan[2] and built the Afghan sovereign and powerful Kingdom[3] in 1747. He had a dream of strong and growing Afghanistan in various aspects of political, social, cultural and economic dimension. In order to achieve his goal and make his dream come true he implemented 'adaptive and maladaptive' strategies.[4] He brought together all Afghans and especially the Pashtuns or Pashto speaking people and tribes.[5] Ahmad just after three years had control over the Hindukush located between the Indus and Oxus rivers. But after his death in 1773

Afghanistan faced huge crisis because of the struggle for power. At the meantime the British made their way in most parts of the India and expanding their governance till Sutlej. Destructive fighting brought in Amir Dost Mohammad Khan to Political stream and power in Afghanistan by 1826. He also carried the same intension of Ahmad Shah and followed his path of strengthening and expanding the Afghan empire towards Peshawar. To achieve his aim he called upon the British but they rejected his request[6] being alone Ranjit Singh defeated him in 1837.[7] Captain Brunes, was sent by Lork Aukland in a mission to check the advancement of Persia[8] and Russia, and also to make peace between Amir Dost Mohammad Khan and Ranjit Singh but the Afghan Amir lost his trust on British and turned towards Russia to gain more benefit than the British.[9]

In order to monitor the hostile actions of Persia and Russia, the British government was interested to install a puppet government in Afghanistan.[10] Shah Shuja the removed Afghan ruler living in exile in UK was brought back by British to the political scene and for his restoration a trilateral treaty was signed between Ranjit Singh and Shah Shuja and the British government.[11] After launching a war against Afghanistan in 1839 Shah Shuja was named the governor of Khandahar. Amir was captivated in Peshawar.[12]

The Afghan people were against British such schemes and disliked the Shah Shuja and as a result of a small clash Shah Shuja was killed in Kabul[13] and as a result Governor-General, Lord Ellenborough, was succeeded by Lord Auckland in 1842. The Amir was released and the Afghan were given the choice to select any government.[14] At the meantime Ranjit Singh power extended up to the east of Khyber,[15] and after the collapse of Sikh empire the British controlled the territory and were to able have a direct contact with the Afghan territory.[16] Afghanistan borders were not clearly defined in that time which caused the strained of relations between British and Russians.[17] As the British dominance and control over the region expanded Russia was also following the similar path which made it difficult for British. The British knew that Afghanistan without any defined territory is the country between their empire and Russia and also having direct control over Afghanistan was difficult because of the mountainous region and the people of Pastuns who love independence so Britain wanted to have an independent Afghanistan to counter Russia.[18] So the British made Afghanistan a buffer state between British India and the Russia, and Afghanistan as victim between two great powers.[19] The annexation of Sikh possession tensed the relations between Afghanistan and the British India in 1849 because the territory was claimed by both sides. The British claimed the territory ruled by Ranjit Singh directly comes under their rule as property. This situation existed till 1883 because the issue of borders settlement was postponed by one or another side. After the death of Singh the relations between British and Sikhs deteriorated and Amir Dost Mohammad Khan took the Benefit of the situation and again took control of Peshawar valley. Amir Dost Muhammad Khan posted his son Ghulam Haider Khan to Peshawar and signed an agreement in 1855 which the both side agreed to respect each other territories. The Amir affirmed himself as 'the friend of friends and enemy of enemies of the Honorable East India Company.' Haider Khan was interested to identify the boundaries of Afghanistan with the British government unclear reply 'the present boundaries of Afghanistan are, of course, those which well be maintained."[20]

The Indo-Afghan frontiers witnessed problems in 1857 when Amir Dost Muhammad Khan persuaded the governor of Peshawar and Kashmir on Swat and Bajaur to Afghanistan territory.[21] The British cautioned both sides for their designs and started their own plans the Khyber tribes to use the Khyber Pass, which was claimed by the Afghans. So, Swat, Bajaur and Khyber Pass was claimed by Afghan Amir. The action was in contradiction with the 1855 treaty.[22] Amir Dost Mohammad beside all the obstacles strived for merging and strengthening his empire on western side. In 1863, he took the possession of Herat which after one month the Amir passed away. Amirs' third son Sher Ali Khan took the reign but struggle for power made it difficult for Amir Dost Mohammad Khan sons to be united.[23] The Governor General of India John Lawrence in order to make friendship with Afghan government recognised Sher Ali Khan as the ruler of Afghanistan accepted the Indus as a line of defence and proposed Peshawar, Kohat and Derajat conceded to Amir.[24] John Lawrence assure Sher Ali Khan if the British attempted to keep away Kashmir and Peshawar from Afghanistan, the Afghans have the right to find any ally to take those regions back till Indus.[25] The plan by Lawrence was made to counter the Russian influence and advancement.

Amir Abdur Rahman Khan took the power from Sher Ali Khan in 1866 but after two years Sher Ali Khan took the region and soon after holding the power he expressed interest for an interview with Viceroy Eral of Mayo that took place in 1869 Ambala which the British government committed itself and assured Amir Abdur Rahaman Khan of any support if Amir observed any malicious acts from his rivals.[26] The scheme for support was to have control over the ruler of Afghanistan and also to keep Sher Ali away from the Russians. In 1872, Lord Mayo was assassinated by a pathan[27] succeeded by Lord Northbook. It was the time when Russia made advancement towards the northern frontiers of Afghanistan.

The Shimla meeting held in 1873 between the Afghan envoy and Lord Northbook main aim was to have British support in case of any attack by Russia on Afghanistan because the Afghans expressed great concern over the rapid movement of Russia in Central Asia which the assurance of the support was renewed by Northbook given before by Lord Mayo.[28] So till 1874 the British government pursued the 'masterly-inactivity' but change of government by bringing conservative party changed the policy to 'aggressive intervention' by Lord Lytton the new viceroy.[29] Relations witnessed strained between Sher Ali and British government not only because of British imperialist policy but also Russia's rise on the western frontier. In 1874, Sir Bartle Frere, member of the Indian Council asked for active interference in Afghanistan on stationing British Officers and agents and advance posts, to compel Amir to confer with British government on her foreign policy.[30] The forward policy of British took more practical steps in 1877 by Lord Lytton occupying Quetta which his expansionist policy was also criticised in Great Britain. The Times wrote 'judicious to make an advance into Baluchistan' over which 'Afghanistan has some historical claims to take an interest....'[31] After the incident it was in July 1878 Kabul witnessed receiving a Russian delegation. A similar agreement was made to send a British party but according to the orders of Amir the British envoy was refused to travel through the Khyber Pass. It was by 20 November 1878 the British government threatened the Amir for war if not supported and accepted the demands made by them. After the clear response from the Amir the British army crossed the frontier through Khandhar and Sher Ali after several defeats fled to Turkistan in 1878. When the British knew that the Amir died so they started talks with Yakub Khan, the son of Amir, that later signed the Gandamk treaty was in May 1879.[32] Based on the treaty Yakub Khan agreed to conduct his foreign relations through British government.[33] The British through this agreement have the control over the Khyber and Michini Passes. The British side agreed to support the Amir Yakub Khan against foreign attacks and an annual subsidy of 6 lakh.[34] But the freedom loving Afghan nation rejected the Gandamk treaty and killed the British resident which resulted in British retaliation attack on Khandhar. The British also forced Yakub Khan to seek refuge in India. This encouraged Lytton to continue his scheme for dividing Afghanistan that later proved to be unsuccessful[35] as his mission completed in June 1880.

Lord Ripon successor of Lytton as new Viceroy to India was to bring normalcy to the Anglo-Afghan relations from the policy of aggression and war of Lytton. To strengthen the relations and as sign of friendship the British government accepted the nephew of Amir Sher Ali as the Amir of Kabul with the assurance taken from Amir not joining any alliance and British also pledged of any required assistance to Amir.[36] It was also made clear with the Amir that the Michini and Khyber Pass were to be controlled by British government. Amir Abdur Rahman Khan in order to maintain his rule as the Amir of Afghanistan accepted the governemnet of India proposal on 1 August 1880.[37] With the provision of annual subsidy of Rs 12 lakhs to Amir the British further cemented its ties and assurance of assistance.[38] The money was to be spent on military expenses for the protection of the north-west frontier so to prevent the Russian advancement in Central Asia. The British policy witnessed no change towards the frontier tribes during the Ripon's rule. The Afridi tribe control was given to the Governor of Punjab because the Afghan Amir claiming sovereignty on that area.

Independent tribes between Afghanistan and British India were helpful in restoration of good neighbourly relations according to Lord Ripon. The action created a buffer zone between Afghanistan and the British India Company as Afghanistan itself was a buffer between two empires of Russia and Britain. The expansionism Policy of Lord Ripon on tribes of the Frontier caused doubts to Amir as he was eager to have the area under his control due to Islamic influence in the area so to build his spiritual authority. Amir Abdur Rahman appealed if the tribes were under his control through him it will protect the British interest and if left independent wouldn't help the British government in case of any required assistance.[39] So both Amir of Afghanistan and the British government strived to maintain their influence among the tribes during 80's.

In 1872-73, British and Russia, signed the agreement of Clarendon-Gortchakoof on the north-western frontier of Afghanistan without the presence of Afghan Amir.[40] The Russians got the control over Merv[41] and advanced towards the Herat. The British government made it clear that any act would have its consequences. British also called upon the Amir to stand with them on the conditions offered to him including the conduct of his foreign relations or else the British government carries no responsibility of protecting Afghanistan.

Amir had no option but to accept the British government because of the Russian advancement in the region and he was not in favour of any British or Russia in his Kingdom affairs.[42] The Amir on the position of Afghanistan said; a goat between two lions or that of a grain of wheat between two strong millstones of the grinding mill.[43]

Russia and England commenced talks over the demarcation of the north-west frontier of Afghanistan, and the Amir agent responsible to inform Amir on any decision point in the meeting[44] was not accepted as commissioner but as representative of his highness and an advisor to the British commissioner. The act made the Amir concerned and declared his independence in external affairs. "I will never consent to the meeting being convened without the presence of the officials of the God granted government."[45] The Amir also in response to the British government said: "they did not allow us to join in the meeting in which discussions were held in regard to delimitation of our and the Russian frontiers."[46] He has further added even if the decision was in favour of Afghan where our honour is while our representative is not present: "where the honour of the Afghan government is if the Commissioner of the two governments should hold discussions about our house, while the owners of the house are not present."[47] Besides all the remarks and protests the demarcation line was drawn in July 1887. After six years, in 1892 dispute started between the British government and Russia over the whole of Pamirs.[48] But the understanding between both British and Russian government made it easy.

Lord Rippon didn't believe in 'buffer-state' policy.[49] Lord Rippons actions made the Amir to be more confident for

Afghanistan independence. Amir Abdur Rahman in his remarks to the Afghan people said: 'if at any time the British think of annexing Afghanistan, he will be the first person to oppose them'. So Amir Abdur Rahman was vigorously striving to have his influence in tribal areas and that made the British to confirm the Indo-Afghan frontier.

Sir Henry Mortimer Durand proposed by Lord Dufferin for the first time was sent in a mission to Kabul in 1888.[50] But due to several reasons the mission was postponed. The Amir for six years rejected any British mission because of the concerns he had from the British government schemes. Hence he adopted 'dilatory tactics.'[51] During the period of 1888-1993 the Amir wanted to get together all Pakhtoons from Baluchistan in the South and from Bajaur in the north. Amir Abdur Rahman Khan in a talk with the British agent said:

> There are several outlaying parts of my dominion with which I have not hitherto interfered, as I did not think worthwhile; but now that the extent of my possession has been called in question, the duty of asserting my authority, so as to settle the matter, has become incumbent on the dealing with those places are to be regarded as internal affairs of Afghanistan.[52]

The Amir illustrated that all tribal areas are part of Afghanistan[53] which his way of thinking was in full contradiction with the British. Later Lord Dufferin was succeeded by Lord Landowne in December 1888. He believed on rapid integration of tribes with the British India as they may join the Afghan side.[54] So he practiced forward policy. His remarks on the tribal territory were:

> The Sphere of influence, within which we shall not attempt to administer the country ourselves, but within which we shall not allow any aggression or interference from without.[55]

In 1892, the British government called it would send a mission under the Lord Roberts to Afghanistan to demarcate the boundary between Afghanistan and British but the Amir refused to accept the mission and also he was busy in Hazara affairs. The Amir also recognised the issue importance and that should be discussed with the tribal elders. Amir Abdur Rahman Khan also refused to visit India as he was invited by the viceroy he thought of keeping down his level to an Indian Raja. He also made it clear to the British that he has kept pledges committed before them beside pressure from Russia but still the British government wants proof from him on territories. He asked 'what greater proof is required than that they go by the name of Afghanistan and not India.'[56] He also opposed the British government's efforts to undermine his power vis-à-vis the Russians. He warned that this situation could be injurious to the British interest also. After the reactions shown by the Amir of Afghanistan the British government stopped the assistance of ammunition to Amir so to force him for table talks and to accept the British proposal on the north-western frontier. Amir Abdur Rahman Khan had no options but to accept the demands of British government he asked the British government:

> 'Where is the frontier line of Afghanistan? Make up your minds and let me know the worst.' Afghan Amir such remarks was a clear manifestation of how he was under immense pressure and finally declared to accept the British mission.

It was Sir Henry Mortimer Durand, selected by the British government to find a solution for the Afghan-Indo frontier. He had also been given the authority to talk and compromise wherever required. The wording of the instructions given to Durand was indeed sharp and indicative that the British were keenly conscious of the Fact that the Afghan Chief Abdur Rahman owes to us his throne and the resources which had enabled him to maintain it and that he has no right whatever to resent any action that we may see fit to take with regard to the tribes and countries which we never handed over to him and which from no part of his dominion.[57]

Days before the arrival of British mission, the Amir published pamphlets in Kandahar proclaimed himself to be independent from the British government. It can be interpreted as it was indirect warning to British not to go against his wish or it was for the people that he will not sacrifice Afghanistan's independence. The Amir in his talks with the British agent made it clear that any foreigner meddling in Afghanistan affairs is treated as enemy by the Afghan people.[58] It was on November 1893 that Durand signed two agreements with Amir Abdur Rahman. It's believed that Durand was able to clear all uncertainties and convinced the Amir.

Based on the first agreement Afghan Amir lost control over all district to the north of upper Oxus, to the South of the river[59] while based on the second agreement Amir was given the control of Kunar, Asmar and Birmal areas respectively. The Amir also pledged not to interfere in Chitral, Bajaur and Swat and given up his desire for Chagai, Dawar and Waziristan.

In order to strengthen the relations with the Amir the British as part of their scheme also increased the amount of subsidy by Rs 6 lakhs, Durand said: "to mark their sense of friendly spirit in which the Amir had enter into negotiations." Durand successfully implemented his mission and in some aspects has gone even beyond and he was able to have Amir Abdur Rahman friendship and goodwill.[60]

Amir Abdur Rahman Khan also said:

> I am glad to have secured for you a good friend in the British Government, our interests and terms are identical. They have no evil designs on your country and are always real to help Afghanistan in its difficulties...[61]

Durand also said that both governments have come to understand and for strengthening of friendship. It's also believed that the Amir has also expressed his contentment on the agreement and hoped for the continuation of Afghan-British alliance. The Indo-Afghan border was demarcated in November 1893 except Khyber and Mohmand.[62] But after wards the Durand agreement seemed to have failed in finding a solution to the founder. The tribe called the agreement as interference into their independence and they also feared from the annexation of their area by the British. The Amir also in 1986 expressed his dissent over the map drew by the British but British put the pressure on Amir to accept it. In 1897 the two tribes of Waziri and Afridi started uprising. After the signing of agreement it drew different views on the Durand Line. The Afghans called it as 'Unequal treaty' forced by British on Afghanistan. Fraser Tytler a well known writer defines the Durand Line as 'the concrete symbol of compromise, the manifestation of a policy which, whatever its merits, was not carried to its logical conclusion."[63] He besides the advantages of line regarded as illogical because of ethnography, strategy and geography as it divides tribes from the both sides of the border.[64] Another expert also observed:

> The new boundary line was not based upon sound topographical data, for during the process of demarcation, it was discovered that certain places, marked on Durand Map, did not exist on the actual ground. Many ethnic absurdities were perpetrated ... The worst blunder of all was the arrangement by which the boundary cut the Mohmand tribal areas into two separate parts.[65]

Edward Thompson and G.T. Garrant also had views: 'while not satisfactory from the Amir's point of view, was also drawn without consulting the tribes affected.'[66] Sir Percy Sykes wrote: "Durand...did not propose to move forward the administrative border of India, but merely pushed for political control."[67] An Indian newspaper because of subsidy given to the Amir by the Indian tax payers called it as burden and criticised the agreement.[68] In the meantime some leaders and writers called it as satisfactory. The Times (London) wrote: "satisfactory settlement of a number of outstanding questions."[69]

Lord Lansdowne and Curzon called it a great success and victory for Durand diplomacy. Meanwhile Amir Abdur Rahman several times protested on the frontier issue and asked the tribal areas to be under his rule. Although, the call made by the Amir was rejected many times by the British but Afghan aspiration to include east of the Durand Line with Afghanistan remained alive. The situation laid negative consequences on the border and strained of relations between Afghanistan and British India even after the independence of Pakistan and still exists between the two neighbouring countries of Afghanistan and Pakistan.[70]

Habibullah, successor of Amir Abdur Rahman came to power in 1901, he also followed his father path and resisted against the British that further deteriorated the relations between the two countries. The British had no option but to cut the subsidy which angered Habibullah and reacted with a question while the British government refuses to pay the subsidy then there is no longer valid, was not also the Durand Agreement?[71] The query was difficult to be answered by the British government. A mission was sent to Kabul under Louis Dane, Foreign Secretary of the Government of India, in 1904. Habibullah continued protesting against the British for their behaviour and didn't accept the treaties that were signed between his father and the British government.[72]

The British and Russians signed 1907 convention in St. Petersburg based on the agreement Russian expressed that Afghanistan was no more to be under the area of their power and talks on Afghan-Russian relations to be held with British. It was also made clear in the agreement that the British had no right to seize or annex any area of Afghanistan. Afghan Amir discarded the convention and this turned to intensify the already worsen relations between the British and the Afghan Amir. It was due to British such schemes that frontiers in the next two years witnessed conflicts in Afridi and Mohmands valley in 1908.[73] The British in order to maintain their control over the tribes started military attacks.[74] To find solution to the problems confronted by the frontier the Amir proposed a joint commission in 1909.[75] First World War started and the suggestion made by Amir Habibullah stayed behind. The Amir took a clever decision of neutrality in the war which British rewarded him with increase in subsidy in 1916.[76] But the Amir interest seemed to be much more than expected by the British and it was not only freedom in conducting of external relations but also control over the frontier area that resulted in third Anglo-Afghan war aimed to protect frontier Pakhtoons from British.

Sardar Amanullah son of Amir Habibullah came to power after his father was killed in February 1919 and proclaimed Afghanistan independence in both external and internal affairs.[77] Afghans main aim and wish for treaty with the British was that Pakhtoon tribal areas should be under Afghanistan rule.[78] It was the Rawalpindi Treaty signed on 08 August 1919 that brought peace and also the British recognised Afghanistan independence in foreign relations. To find solution for frontier problem the Amir proposed talks to be held between the representatives of both Afghan and British which negotiations went up to two years and finally the outcome was Anglo-Afghan treaty signed on 21 November 1921. The Afghan representative called the talks as very tough:

> We do not see the object of these long discussions. We wish to get to the point. The truth is this, we can still make a good bargain with Bolsheviks, but we prefer to deal with Great Britain ... if they (Bolsheviks) will offer us enough, we must turn to the Bolsheviks. There is still time to do so. But also we require Waziristan. The British Government must be tired of trying to restrain these tribes and we could keep them in much better order.[79]

Dobbs, the British representative was assigned to talk about an agreement in Mussoorie aide-memoire that based on the accord Afghanistan to maintain neighbourhood and wouldn't authorise along the frontier border any Russian consulate.[80] It was a worst choice as it created obstacles before the strengthening of relations between Afghanistan and its Southern neighbours. Amir Ammanullah due to domestic crisis approved the agreement and recognised the existed Afghan-Indo frontier[81] and British also accepted Afghanistan's officially free and independent in its internal and external affairs.[82] The Amir called the agreement as to strengthen the friendly neighbourhood relations not as friendly treaty. The unrest and the deteriorating of situation in tribal areas of frontier made it difficult for British to convince Afghan King on recognising the Durand Line as the international boundary which till the last the British failed in their mission. Ammanullah after the independence started the reform process in the country but his endeavours witnessed great resistance and he was forced to leave the country in January 1929. It was Nadir Khan that after months of conflict controlled the situation in October 1929.[83] Finally, the British formally recognised Afghanistan on 15 November 1929 and in 1930 memorandums were changed to further strengthen the relations between Afghanistan and British and to confirm the Afghan-Anglo agreement of 1921.[84] But there was no change of policy seen from the British towards the frontier. Besides the Simon Commission report (1928-30) that "British India stops at the boundary of the administered area,"[85] the British pursued their meddling in frontier and through military operations resisted against the Afridis and Mahsuds in 1930-31 also in Waziristan uprising of 1936-38. Afghans were thinking of recapturing the tribal areas after the departure of British. It was in 1931-32 table conference that Afghanistan called on British to take the Afghan government in confidence while taking any decision on the area. During the Cripps Mission visit to India the Amir again asked for the solution of the issue but the British side called the Afghan government appeal to be taken in appropriate time into account.[86] Although Afghanistan had warm relations with Germany but kept her neutrality in Second World War and after the war British was no longer to keep its rule over the area so the Kabul government called on British to let the people of area on their choice either to join with Afghanistan or be independent. But the British never bothered to think about the proposal made by the Afghan government instead they pursued their own plan on 3 June 1947 either to join with Pakistan or India.

A well known Pakhtoon leader of frontier Khan Abdul Ghaffar Khan in a letter to Gandhi on 11 June 1947 asked him for Pakhtoons choice between Pakistan and a free state of Pathan but the British government refused to accept the proposal made by the Khan. To know what the people for frontier want a referendum was held but Congress being in majority boycotted because they didn't want the frontier to be separated and independent. In spite of this from 286370 voted for Pakistan and only 2974 votes were in favour of India.[87]

References

1. Fraser Tytler has summarised the various theories about the origin of the Pakhtoons. See for details W.K. Fraser Tytler, *Afghanistan: A study of Political Development in Central Asia* (London, Oxford University Press, 1950), p. 47.
2. This had been expressed in the "Will of Peter the Great". See for the text Percy Sykes, History of Persia (London, Macmillan, 1951), Vol. II pp. 244 and 246.
3. Ganda Singh, "Ahmed Shah Durani: Father of Modern Afghanistan," (Bombay, Asia Publishing House, 1959), p. 36.
4. According to Abdur Rahman, the Amir of Afghanistan, it was in 1747, that the history of Afghanistan made a start in having an elected and constitutional type of government, then the various tribes had elected Ahmed Shah as their king, See Abdur Rahman, "the Life of Abdur Rahman Amir of Afghanistan," ed., Mir Munshi Sultan Mohammed Khan (London, Murray, 1990) Vol. II, p. 215.
5. Joseph Frankel, "Contemporary International Theory and the Behaviour of States," (London Oxford University Press 1973), p. 45.
6. W.K. Fraser, pp. 63-64. However, in an attempt to arrange a settlement of the Punjab, Ahmed Shah recognised in 1762 the Mogul Prince Shah Alam II as Emperor at Delhi, while in 1767 he gave up the Central Punjab to the Sikhs, retaining under his control Peshawar and the Northern Punjab. Thus, his empire

started crumbling during his own life time. However, according to another reliable sources, it is stated that even at the beginning of the 19th century, the Durani empire extending from Herat to Kashmir and from Balkh to Sind, which had been built by Ahmed Shah, remained undivided in the hands of his grandson, Zaman Shah, which was however divided in the following years of Political Confusion, when Ranjit Singh annexed the valley of Peshawar. See for detail C.U. Aitcheson, *A Collection of Treaties, Engagements and Sanads in Relation to India and Neighbouring Countries*, (Calcutta, Government of India Central Publication Branch, 1933, Reprint, 1973), Vol. Xiii, part II, pp. 203-204. Here after referred as Aitcheson Treaties.

7. J.D. Cunningham, *A History of the Sikhs*, (New Delhi, S. Chand, 1972), p. 188.
8. In fact it was a matter of grave concern for Auckland, when Muhammad Shah, king of Persia, laid siege to Herat in pursuance of his ambitious policy for the reconquest of Afghanistan with aid and advice of Russia.
9. Aitcheson Treaties, n.10, p. 2015.
10. *Ibid.* It was this objective of the British government which was advanced to Justify Auckland policy of Anglo Afghan war and approved by the Secret Committee. This was also evident from the manifesto which appeared under the signature of the Secretary of State, Macnaghten. See for details W.K. Fraser, n.04, p. 110.
11. Aitcheson Treaties, n.10, Vol. 1, pp. 41-44.
12. *Ibid.,* Vol. XIII, part II, p. 205.
13. The Afghan Policy of Lord Auckland had earned universal condemnation at the hands of almost all the critics and he was soon recalled to his country.
14. Aitcheson Treaties, n. 10, Vol. 01, p. 205.
15. Ganda Singh, n. 04, p. 71.
16. L.B. Polullada, "Pushtunistan: Afghan Domestic Politics and Relations with Pakistan," in A.T. Embreee, ed., *Pakistan Western Borderlands*, (New Delhi, Vishal, 1977), p. 129.
17. *Ibid.*
18. Ludwig W. Adamec, *Afghanistan 1990-1923: A Diplomatic* History (Berkeley, University of California Press, 1976), p. 17.
19. Neville Maxell, *India's China War*, (Bombay, Jaico Publishing House, 1950), pp. 20-23.
20. For. Dept. Sec. Cons., N.A.I., June 1855, No. 53.
21. For. Dept. Sec. Cons., N.A.I., June 1858, No. 06.

22. Aitcheson Treaties, n.10, p. 237. The British government had given a general pledge and assurance to Ghulam Haider Khan that it would respect the territory of Afghanistan.
23. *Ibid,* p. 208.
24. W.W. Hunter, Life of Earl of Mayo, Vol. I, p. 284.
25. Lawrence Papers, Lawrence to Sir Bartle Frere, N.A.I., 28 June 1866.
26. Aitcheson Treaties, n. 10, p. 209.
27. P.E. Reberts, n. 41, pp. 414-415.
28. *Ibid.,* p. 245.
29. C.C. Davies, n. 42, p. 156.
30. D.K. Ghose, n. 56, pp. 11-13.
31. The Times, 5 November 18777 as cited in D.K. Ghose, n 56, pp. 17-18.
32. For text of Treaties see Aitcheson Treaties, n. 10, pp. 240-242.
33. *Ibid.,* also see, Arnold Fletcher, Afghanistan: Highway of Conquest (New York, Cornell University Press, 1965), pp. 246-247.
34. Aitcheson Treaties, *Ibid.*
35. Hasan Kakar, "Afghanistan from Disintegration to reunification: 1880-1884," Afghanistan. Vol. XXIII, No. 1, 1970, pp. 13-14.
36. Aitcheson Treaties, n. 10, p. 212. Also see, C.C. Davies, n. 42, p. 157.
37. Aitcheson Treaties, n. 10, pp. 212-213.
38. *Ibid.,* p. 213.
39. For Dept. Sec. F Progs., Nos. 573-580, Letters from the Amir to Mr. Payne relating to the differences with his Highness in regard to Indo-Afghan frontier, N.A.I.A. August 1893, N. 576.
40. Aitcheson Treaties, n.10, pp. 214-218.
41. Dept. Sec. F Progs., Nos1-10, Letters from agent in Baluchistan to the Secretary to the Government of India, N.A.I. March 1885 no. 515C.
42. Dept. Sec. F, n. 81, No. 248.
43. Abdur Rahman, n.07, p. 280.
44. Lt. Col. J.W. Rideggeway to H.M. Durand, D.O, dated 21 December 1884, Fore, Dept. Sec F Progs. Nos. 187-326 A, N.A.I., February 1885.
45. A note from H.M. Durand to his Excellency, the Viceroy, dated 13 February 1885, For Dept Sec., F. Progs. Nos. 187-326 A, N.A.I., February 1885.

46. A letter from his Highness the Amir of Afghanistan, Ghazi Sad-ud-Din Khan,dated 7 January 1885, No. 310 A.
47. A note from his Highness the Amir of Afghanistan to Ghazi Sad-ud-Din Khan,dated 7 January 1885, n. 88, No. 310A.
48. For Details of Pamir Crisis G.K. Alder, n. 50, pp. 248-262.
49. Dufferin papers, Dufferin to Churchill, 30 July 1885.
50. Dufferin Papers Dufferin to cross, 10 August 1888.
51. See for details For. Dept. Sec. F. Progs., Nos. 67-91, N.A.I., April 1893, No. 67.
52. A Note from A.E. Miller to his Excellency, the viceroy, dated 4 May 1893, For Dept. Sec. F Progs., Nos. 312-314. N.A.I., June 1893 (K.W.), no. 1, No. 312.
53. A note from H.M. Duran to his Excellency, the Viceroy, dated 1 May 1893, *Ibid.*
54. Lansdowne Paper, Lansdowne to Robert, 17 February 1889.
55. Cited in P.E. Roberts, n. 41, p. 487. Also see For. Dept Sec. F Prog., Nos. 67-91, N.A.I., April 1893, No. 70.
56. Leter from his Highness, the Amir of Afghanistan to Mr. Pyne, dated 15 July 1893, for Dept. Sc., F. Progs., Nos. 573-58, N.A.I., August 1893, No. 573.
57. For. Dept. Sec. F. Progs., nos. 573-580. N.A.I., August 1893, No. 575.
58. Peshawar Confidential Diary, No. 19, dated 23 September 1893, For Dept. Sec., F. Progs., Nos. 175-183, N.A.I., November 1893, No. 175 (Kabul Mission-1).
59. Aitchison Treaties, n. 10. p. 218. For the text of treaty see pp. 255-256. Also see For. Dept. Sec. F. Prog., Nos. 159-199. N.A.I., December 1893, No. 160.
60. Kabul Mission diary, 12-16 November 1893, For dept., Sec., F Prgs., Nos. 71-158, N.A.I., December 1893, No. 154.
61. *Ibid.*
62. Aitchison Treaties, n.10, p. 129.
63. W.K. Fraser Tytler, n.04, p.188. also cited by R.H.K., "The Durand Line," *Afghanistan News*, Vol. V, No. 62, October 1962, p. 17.
64. W.K. Fraser Tytler, *Ibid.*
65. C.C. Davies, n.42, pp.161-162. The writer viewed that the Amir's consent was brought by increase of his subsidy and by the recognition of his right import munitions of war.
66. Edward Thompson and G.T. Garratt, Rise and Fulfilment of British Rule in India (London, Oxford University Press 1925), p. 553.

67. Sir Percy Sykes, N.76, p. 219.
68. The Bengaleee, 25 November 1893.
69. The Times, 30 December 1893.
70. L.F. Rushbrook Williams, the State of Pakistan (London, Faber and Faber 1966), pp. 62-63.
71. For Dept. Sec F Progs., Nos. 13-14, N.A.I., February 1903, No. 14.
72. Aitcheson treaties, n.10, pp. 282-283.
73. C.C. Davies, n.42, p.173.
74. Harm J. De Blij, n.03, p.199.
75. Aitcheson Treaties, n.10, p. 22.
76. *Ibid.*
77. Aitcheson Treaties, n.10, pp. 222-223.
78. For. Dept Front B Progs., Nos. 15-138, N.A.I., October 1919, No. 78.
79. For. Dept Front B Progs., Nos. 317-550, N.A.I., October 1920, No. 453.
80. Ludwig, W. Adame, n. 143, p. 160.
81. Aitcheson Treaties, n. 10, p. 225.
82. Olof Caroe, The Pathans, 550 B.C.-1957 A.D. (London, Oxford University Press, 1965), p. 464.
83. Aitcheson Treaties, N. 10, pp. 230-231.
84. *Ibid.*
85. Cited in Louis Dupree, n. 150, p. 487.
86. 'Conflicts in Pakhtunistan,' The Egyptian Economic and Political Review, October 1955, p. 11.
87. M.A. Chaudhri, 'The Relations of Pakistan with Afghanistan,' Pakistan Horizon, Vol.viii, No. 04 December 1955, p. 496.

CHAPTER - IV

PASTUNISTAN: AFGHANISTAN, PAKISTAN AND PASTUN PERSPECTIVE

It is important to know about the concept of Pakhtoonistan prior to the opinions of both neighbouring countries of Afghanistan and Pakistan on the issue. Pakistan has visualised the Pakhtoonistan as 'hypothetical state.'[1] The definition available from three different sources prevail it as the Afghans, the Pakhtoons living outside Pakistan and the Pakhtoons inside Pakistan. Afghan government since the Durand Line signed in 1893 till now believe and mention Pakhtoonistan areas covering two provinces of Baluchistan and North West Frontier recently known as Khyber Pakhtoonwah.[2] A well known Afghan diplomat writes that Pakhtoonistan comprise areas of Chitral, Hazara, Khohistan, Swat, Dir, Buner, Peshawar, Tirah, Bajaur, Kohat, Bannu, Dera Ghazi Khan, Dera Ismail Khan, Waziristan, Khyber, Pezu, Gomal, Bolan, and Malakand.[3]

Khan Ghazi Kabuli another prominent scholar hints that Pakhtoonistan includes areas of Gilgit, to the Arabian Sea and from the Durand Line to Muzaffarabad on Kashmir boundary. Kabuli stated Pakhtoonistan as independent and sovereign state outside Pakistan.[4] But the Pakhtoon leaders like Khan Abdul Gaffar Khan and Wali Khan defined Pakhtoonistan area as NWFP recently named Khyber Pakhtoonwah to be called after Pakhtoons and autonomous region within the Pakistan. Pakistan's total area is 39259 square miles divided into tribal territory and settled districts. The Pashtu or Pakhto[5] language is known as the identity of Pakhtoon living in Pakhtoonistan but some place not resided by Pakhtoons, Pashtu is not spoken. The Pakhtoonistan issue has played a major role in Afghanistan's foreign policy and it's vital to know the Afghanistan stand on the issue.

Afghanistan Perspective

Afghans assert and claim Pakhtoonistan because of the ethnic, linguistic, geographical, historical, traditional aspect and more over the Pakhtoons are akin to them. Afghans believe that the Durand Line was imposed on Afghan Amir Abdur Rahman and he signed the treaty with British because he was under immense internal and external pressure.[6] They also believe the drawn of line as illogical and unacceptable that compulsorily divided blood brothers from each other.[7] 'British did a wrong many years ago and we have been fighting to rectify it. Until that is done the struggle will continue.'[8]

The NWFP destiny remained unclear during the partition based on referendum. The Afghan government called the referendum as unacceptable and not a logical way to solve the issue. The reason for the decision of referendum as invalid by the Afghan side was that it was only taken by the British ignoring the other parties considerations and decisions and it was not a good step taken by British because it didn't talk about the Pakhtoons to be part of their motherland or to have their own independent state but instead to be part of India or Pakistan.

And it was reflected in the referendum as it was boycotted and the tribal people didn't even cast their votes.[9] It signified their interest for independence or to unite with their motherland and was against the referendum. The Frontier

Gandhi Khan Abdul Ghaffar Khan in his remarks on 'Pakhtunistan Day' 1 September 1967 said:

> ...Field Marshal Ayub Khan claimed that a referendum was held in North-West Frontier Province before the creation of Pakistan. I strongly repudiate it. The farce of referendum was staged by the British government: first, on issues we are not interested in: second, based on limited franchise: third, with no supervision and control of the ballots: forth, rigging of votes and fifth, non-participation by majority of Pashtoons.[10]

Also the Afghan government in a statement called the referendum as "fraud and a shame"[11] Mohammad Ali an Afghan scholar and writer in his book "The Durand Line" writes that historians and geographers has been the Indus as right ethnological boundary between India and Afghanistan but disregarded by British. The Afghan government after the elections refused to accept the outcome and also Pakistan officials' remarks that Pakhtoons with their determination has freely chosen Pakistan. Therefore, the Afghan government called for self-determination of Pakhtoons living in Pakistan. After the formation of Pakistan it applied for United Nations membership that Afghanistan voted against Pakistan. The Afghan representative in UN, Hosyan Azizi in his remarks in General Assembly said:

> We cannot recognise the North-West Frontier as part of Pakistan so long as people of the North-West Frontier have not been given opportunity free from any kind of influence and I repeat, free from any kind of influence-to determine for them whether they wish to be independent or to become part of Pakistan.[12]

Since that, it has been Afghan government demand to conduct plebiscite on the Pakistan side of the Durand Line.[13] Najibullah Khan the Afghan ambassador to New Delhi, in his speech on the occasion of "Pakhtoonistan Day" said:

> The Pashtoons are Afghans and it was natural that they should expect Afghanistan to support their cause.

> The government and people of Afghanistan pledged their support to Pushtoons, in doing so Afghanistan is fulfilling not only a natural duty but also helping the cause of justice and peace.[14]

Najibullah Khan Speech based on the principles of UN Charter for a sovereign Pakhtoon state. Afghanistan several times has made it clear that it has not got any expansionist policy or plan irredentist policy and also rejected Pakistan claims over the interference of Afghanistan into internal affairs of Pakistan.[15]

Later the first President of Afghanistan Sardar Daud Khan remarked that his country has no intension to expand its territory and added: "We have certain responsibilities with regard to our Pakhtoon brothers because they are with us in blood and culture."[16] After the oppressive policies of Pakistan government towards the Pakhtoons the Afghan King Zahir Shah in his pointed speech at Afghan National Assembly in 1949 supported the Pakhtoons right to Self-determination. Furthermore the Assembly in a resolution passed rejected and called invalid all agreements, conventions signed between Afghanistan and the British India government also rejected formally the Durand Line.[17] Afghanistan government has repeatedly expressed concern over the Pakhtoon issue and their well being and many times has made it clear to Pakistan that any decision over the future of the tribal areas in Frontier should be based taking into consideration the aspiration of them and Afghanistan would not accept anything different. In 1955, Afghanistan's Grand National Assembly (Loya Jirga) in a resolution refused recognise Pakhtoonistan as part of Pakistan.[18] Meanwhile Rahman Pazhwak strongly discarded the Pakistani government stand that religion is the uniting factor for Pakhtoonistan to be part of Pakistan and further said both India and Pakistan are not purely Muslims or Hindu states.[19] A prominent Afghan Daily while strongly criticised the Pakistan Foreign Minister, M.A. Hussain on his remarks that religion is the factor that has made

Pakhtoonistan to be part of Pakistan.[20] The Saba Kabul wrote:

> It is true as Mr. Hussain says that there can be no difference between Pakistan and Afghanistan, as both are Muslim countries. We would like to ask him whether Islam permits the usurpation of property of a Muslim by another Muhammedan. Does religion prohibit a Muslim from demanding his right from another Muslim? Is it permissible in Islam to commit unlawful murder, to imprison or torture people specifically the Muslims?[21]

Pakistan argument of religion was called as baseless by the Afghan government and was described as aggression and invaders should be opposed. The Afghan government times and again repeatedly expressed protest against the unfair and suppressive plans take on Pakhtoons. Rahman Pazwhak also explicitly said that Pakistan pursues a dual policy on Kashmir and Pakhtoonistan where in Kashmir she is interested to conduct plebiscite but not for Pakhtoonistan. He also stated that Pakistan accepted the result of referendum held by foreign a government but in case of Kashmir though the people of the area in many elections expressed their willingness with India while casting their votes but the Pakistan government didn't accept. Pazwhak also asked for the international community attention on the Pakistani government remarks that President Ayub Khan is Pakhtoon and the Pakhtoon rights are protected as it was not. The Afghan Prime Minister on the occasion of the 50th anniversary of Afghanistan reiterated Afghan government support to Pakhtoon issues and pledged his country's endeavours to find solution for the Pakhtoonistan problem.[22]

The Afghan government always made it clear that she had no intention of interference in Pakistan internal matters but will continue to make efforts for the well being of Pakhtooons and all these attempts are based on the charters of the United Nations to support the Pakhtoons' right to self-determination. Another point raised by Afghanistan was that when British left India the tribal areas or the Pakhtoonistan region was not essential part of any state. Some were administering territories and some other independent tribal areas and based on the international law Pakistan government such action of transformation is 'innovation'.[23] Also Afghanistan because of her security supported the issue as the area is located in border with the country and maintains importance for Afghan nations.[24] Afghanistan couldn't be untouched by the conflict in Pakhtoonistan as it will lay negative consequences and impacts on politics, economy and society. It was a matter of concern for Afghanistan as a landlocked country because of her communication with the outside world and later the Afghan government apprehension proved to be true as the disorder erupted during 1955-1960 in the Pakhtoon area and Afghanistan economy witnessed crisis. In 1973, Daud Khan became the first ever president of Afghanistan and he took the Pakhtoonisatn issue as very serious and said that Pakistan is the only country that Afghanistan has difference of opinion with Pakhtoonistan issue.[25] In his interview he openly said that Afghanistan will not remain unresponsive with injustice continuance in two disturbed provinces of Baluchistan and NWFP and reaffirmed his support to the right of self-determination of Baluchi's and the Pakhtoons and called these movements in these two states as nationalistic in nature to achieve national entity.[26]

Sayid Wahid Adullah the Afghan Deputy Foreign Minister in his remarks said Afghanistan would not remain silent over the Pakistan government recent repressive actions and the use of arms against Pakhtoons and Baluchis.[27] The Afghan government and Afghan leaders expressed willingness to talk with Pakistan over the issue of Pakhtoonistan and solve the issue.[28]

Afghanistan representative to UN Mohammad Pazhwak, in the General Assembly said that Pakhtoonistan is a 'usurped land' that was taken by force by the British colonial master and since that the people of the area resisted, First against British and now against Pakistan for freedom and choice for self-determination. He further said Pakistan's such domination policy is the repetition of British colonialism.[29] Afghan president Daud Khan in a letter to UN secretary on 25 September 1974 supported Baluchi freedom fighters and asked for a investigative team to inspect the area and further said he doesn't carry any plan against the territorial integrity of Pakistan.[30] He again on 25 December same year reiterated for an international commission and accused Pakistan of committing genocide of Baluchis.[31] After the arrest of the Natioanl Awami Party leader and banned on the party in 1975 the Afghan government conveyed its great concern on the issue and called the action as unfairness because without any proof the party leader accused.[32] Afghan government such stand and remarks further deteriorated the relations between two countries. President Daud again wrote to UN Secretary General for the appointment of commission and expressed his concern on increase in the number of refugees to Afghanistan because Pakistan repressive policies. The Pakistan government called Daud's such actions as revoking the opposition to uprising. But the Afghan government repeatedly called the accusations as baseless and the Afghan Foreign Minister Spokesman stated that the claims of Pakistan government express the confused and disturbed situation in Pakistan itself.[33]

The Afghan representative to United Nations Abdullah in 1975 said that the Afghan government strives to solve the problem with Pakistan government with the consideration of Baluch's and the Pakhtoons through talks.[34] This resulted Pakistan government readiness for talks but without any prerequisite. Pakistan made her stand clear that Afghanistan must recognise Durand Line as International border between two neighbouring countries for significant talks.

Afghanistan also left her persistence on the Pakhtoon right to self-determination to be recognised by Pakistan as precondition for everlasting peace between Afghanistan and Pakistan. As a result President Daud and Prime Minister

Bhutto held four days meeting in Kabul on June 1976. The meeting just helped the countries stop propaganda against each other. In August 1976 President Daud in his trip to Pakistan reaffirmed his position on the issue of Pakhtoons and Baluchis and stated the matter could be solved realistically. Bhutoo was ousted from power by General Zia-ul-Haq in July 1977 military coup. Meanwhile President Daud hoped that the change of regime in Pakistan would help the neighbouring countries get closer and find solution to the problem and difference between the two countries.[35] Gen. Zia visit Kabul in October 1977 where Afghan President Daud Khan expressed that the difference would be solved between two countries on mutual understanding and efforts.[36] In March 1978, meetings were held between two leaders where both of them called the result of the meeting as tremendously prolific and helpful on easing of tension in relations between the two neighbours mainly on political differences that strained the relations since thirty years. The last two years relations between Afghanistan and Pakistan reflected ease in relations between two countries on awaited issue of the Pakhtoon and Baluch. After a military coup and the Saur revolution in 1978, the new government Deputy Prime Minister Hafizullah Amin also followed the path of President Daud and expressed Afghan government support to the right of self-determination of Baluch and Pakhtoons. He in his speech delivered in United Nations expressed Afghan government willingness that the issue should be solved through dialogues and taking into consideration the aspirations of Pakhtoons.[37]

Afghan President Noor Mohammad Tarraki in a meeting with Pakistan Premier Zia-ul-Haq in Kabul in 1978 reiterated his country's desire to have friendly relations with Pakistan and find solution to the political differences between the both neighbouring countries through talks.[38] By 1979, it appeared that Afghanistan had flexibility on the Pakhtoonistan issue. The next Afghan government Vice Premier and Foreign Affairs Minister, Hafizullah Amin observed that he would not take it in a way to be misunderstood by the enemies of friendship and brotherhood.[39] The new Afghan government this stand reflected full differences with the before position held and asserted by Taraki and Amin. It's believed that the Afghan government such attitude came based on the reports from the tribal opposition people across the Durand Line that was uprising against the Afghan government. But afterward, Taraki reiterated the Afghan nation and government stand on the Pakhtoons and Baluchs' and will not come under the influence of insurgent groups aided and supported by Pakistan.[40]

Hafizullah Amin the next Afghan President in his first speech expressed he has reviewed Afghan-Pak problems and relations and he will support the Pakhtoonistan issue.[41] The Muslim, 21 September 1979

Soon after the Hafizullah Amin, Babrak Karmal took the power he also supported the right to self-determination of Pakhtoons and Baluch. The new government also expressed readiness to find the solution of the issue through peaceful means and talks. However, Karmal was not succeeded to implement his plans as he was busy in dealing with the insurgencies and uprising against him inside the country. So the conflicts and crisis in Afghanistan has overshadowed the Pakhtoonistan issue but still the issue of Pakhtoons and Baluch and their right to self-determination matters to Afghan people.

The following points can be concluded on Afghanistan stand on Pakhtoonistan issue:

1. The Afghans appealed for the right to self-determination of Pakhtoons beyond the Durand Line. And the Afghan government stated that the Pakhtoon area is under the governing of Pakistan not Kabul.[42]
2. Afghanistan reiterated that she had no interest for territorial expansion because of supporting Pakhtoons and Baluchs.

3. Afghanistan is interested to solve the issue through peaceful talks.
4. And finally Afghanistan wants everlasting solution of the issue with the aspiration of Pakhtoons and Baluchs.

Any Afghan government has supported and never kept silence on the Pakhtoon and Baluch issue because of the presence of extreme Pakhtoon nationalist and their control whose families were separated by the Durand Line. The Afghan government also discarded Pakistan government remarks that annually spend 15 million Rupees for the welfare of Pakhtoon more than the Afghan government total budget.[43] Meanwhile the Afghan government officials called the figures as exaggeration as it was less than one-fifth of Afghanistan budget and this was reflected in life condition of the Pakhtoon. It's while the Baluch and Pakhtoon have expressed concern over the extraction of their natural resources by the Pakistan government.

In brief Afghanistan claims can be summarised into three categories. Historically, it is argued that Afghanistan had under control the recent area under the dispute. Legally, Afghanistan express that the Durand Line treaty in 1893 was signed under pressure and the tribal areas located between Afghanistan and Pakistan were independent. Ethnically, that Afghans and Pakhtoons beyond the Durand Line in Pakistan share same and single ethnicity and by force and illogically have been divided by Durand Line. Therefore, the right to self-determination and protection of Pakhtoons across the border in Pakistan is the obligation and task of Afghanistan to ensure their safety and welfare. The last and the stronger argument is that certain non-Pakhtoon areas are also included in proposed Pakhtoonistan.

Until early 1980s, while Pakistan's Afghan Policy was largely Durand Line Specific, it took a new turn by the end of 1980s. Hoping to establish Mujahideen regime post-Najib government, Islamabad, in fact, the Pakistan military, began to view Afghanistan as backyard it could exploit in many ways. Of course, it is commonly believed that one aim was to maintain Afghanistan as a Source of Strategic Depth in case of possible Indian invasion. Imperial-Style grand Khaki designs for Afghanistan also had in mind its strategic importance for post USSR Central Asia. Likewise, safe havens could be provided for militants trained to wage/ sustain 'Jihad-e-Kashmir'. Perhaps, all of this was not scripted well in advance. The Pakistan Army is hardly known for intelligent planning. However, it turned out to be so. Ironically, neither the Mujahedeen regime, briefly headed by ISI' blue-eyed boy neither Gulbaddin, nor Taliban were ready to submit to Pakistan on the question of Durand Line. Post 9/11, Pakistan lost the Afghan bet, in fact, ever since Afghan chickens returned home to roost. So during Mujahedeen government though Pakistan government and its intelligence service that strongly supported Mujahedeen but was not able to convince them to recognise the Durand Line as the international border between the two neighbouring countries of Pakistan and Afghanistan.

Doubtlessly the Pakistan intelligence agency ISI also sponsored trained and inducted the militant forces which were called the Taliban. The Taliban strength lay in the fact that it was identified with Pakhtoons. This ethnic identity played a significant role in the initial victories of the Taliban over all regional Mujahedeen groups and warlords. Most of its cadres initially were from the Madrassas which had been established by Pakistani fundamentalist political parties like the Jamiat-al-Ulama-i-Islam led by Maulana Fazlur Rahman in the Afghan refugee camps.

Gradually, Pakistan state institutions were deeply involved with Taliban. Pakistan which was on the verge of economic failure in the wake of nuclear tests in the summer of 1998 and yet it was paying a huge amount to the Afghan administration for its upkeep and for the war, above and apart from the funds which were coming from the Saudi and American sources. Islamabad's objectives in creating and nurturing Taliban were that they would recognise the Durand Line, the Taliban regime would work under its influence, and that a friendly Afghanistan would provide access to the newly independent Central Asian Republics and a kind of Islamic bloc would emerge in the region. Pakistan strategies have also talked of Afghanistan providing strategic depth to their country in the event of a confrontation with India although some other deflates the idea. However, the Taliban leadership hardly ever did anything that their mentors in the neighbouring country wanted. The Taliban played one Pakistani institution against other. Its ideology was Deobandi Wahabi interpretation of Islam with a mixture of tribal traditions. The Taliban being Pashtu's did accept the Durand Line and their self-esteem never allowed them to accept subservience to Islamabad.[44] Afghanistan's former President, Hamid Karzai in his remarks called the Durand Line as Line of Hate. He believed the line cutting the tribal territories divides Pashtu's and tribes.[45] Hussain Haqani. Pakistan Ambassador to Washington has said:

> 'People on both sides of the Durand Line consider it a soft border.' He adds, 'Pashtu consider it their own land even though there is also a loyalty to the respective states along the British sphere of influence' (Bajoria, 2009). In an interview to the Radio Liberty, Hamid Karzai said, 'the Afghan and not Hamid Karzai would have to decide the issue of Durand Line'. (Qassem, 2008: 88)

Also in an interview Mohammad Akram Khpalwak the governor of Paktika on April 20, 2007 said RFE/RL's Radio Free Afghanistan that:

> "First of all, we cannot accept the line. It is not demarcated and not clear where the border is. So the Durand Line is the basic issue. For solving the Durand Line issue, the problem of (ethnic-Pashtu) tribes living on both sides should be considered and they must be consulted. So it is very complicated issue and must be determined by the (ethnic-Pashtu) tribes living on both sides of the line."[46]

The Afghan officials have presently asked US for renegotiation of Durand Line. But US has refused to deal with the border issue, rather offered help for the repositioning of small border posts.

Pakistan Perspective

Pakistan government calls the Durand Line treaty signed between Afghanistan and the British as legitimate and official as it was also recognised by the later government of Afghanistan.[47] The Pakistan argument is that the treaty ended Afghanistan's control over the tribal areas and the people inhabited east of the Durand Line.[48]

Pakistan as successor of British Empire took the privilege of all treaties and agreement signed during that time with government and also had the control over the sovereignty of the territory and its inhabitants. In the meantime Pakistan also rejected Afghan government assertion that the treaty was signed under the British influence or pressure.[49] In his remarks the biography of Durand Sir Perey Sykes, said that no forced was used or the Afghan Amir was under any kind of pressure while signing the Durand treaty. He further states to sign the treaty an unarmed mission accompanied Durand to Kabul at the presence of Amir Abdur Rahman[50] and stayed there for four days to discuss the various dimensions of the agreement. The Afghan Amir during the British mission stay in Kabul called a special Darbar where he called praiseworthy the British government plan and even instructed his subjects to treat the British mission as their friends. Amir Abdur Rahman also during the meeting in Darbar offered a paper consisting different Sardars seals that have expressed their trust on the Amir as their ruler.[51] Sir Percy writes if the Afghan and Amir were not interested they would not accept the treaty and were to express their discontent over the treaty. Also if treaty was imposed on Afghans so they were not to express willingness in friendship with British. So their silence on the issue was a proof for acceptance.[52] Meanwhile Pakistan said there has been no prejudices and unfairness in the treaty and there is no question remains to be talked on.

Based on clause of Durand treaty both Afghan and British government have accepted not to middle in each territories issues and all the political differences regarding the frontier issues has been solved "full and satisfactory settlement of all the principal differences of opion which have arisen between them in regard to the frontier."[53] And the Durand Agreement was also accepted as valid by the afterward governments in 1905, 1919, 1921 and 1930.[54] The Pakistani government on the issue of the right to self-determination stated that the British held plebiscite in 1947 which was based on the outcome the majority favoured in North West Frontier Province.[55] In his remarks Pakistan's Minister for Home Affairs in Pakistan National Assembly:

> After all, Sir, is it not satisfactory fact of history that as regards the frontier province, there was a referendum when the Congress Ministry was in power...and in that referendum the people of the Frontier voted for Pakistan Sir, how can that decision of the people be challenged?[56]

The Pakistan government said because the Congress knew they will lose so they raised the issue of Pakhtoonistan.[57] Meanwhile Pakistan government also discarded Afghan government argument that Pakhtoons have given limited choice. Furthermore the Pakhtoons in various occasions have proved their honesty and loyalty with the Pakistan government. A Pakistan writer asserts that the Pakhtoons themselves never has asked for being independent and to annex with Afghanistan so it is more false propaganda.[58] The Pakistan government asserted that the tribal area people through holding of several Jirgas (tribal council)[59] expressed their willingness to be with Pakistan. British Governor of Frontier Province Sir George Cunningham that tribal elders through Jirgas have given him assurance on November 1947 to stay within Pakistan.[60] Liaquat Ali Khan, Prime Minister of Pakistan also said that the tribal areas people in a rational step have expressed their willingness to be part of Pakistan and added 'since then 1947 they have entered into agreement with government of Pakistan by virtue of which their territory has become an integral part of Pakistan.'[61] In view of these belief and contentions, Pakistan attitude towards the Pakhtoonistan question is: *first*, one of puzzlement over what it is supposed to mean as the concept had not been clearly and consistently defined; *secondly*, astonishment that it should be raised at all because Pakistan insists that Afghanistan has no right to speak for the Paktoons living on its side; *thirdly*, Pakistan considers it an offence and deliberate interference in its domestic affairs by Afghanistan for selfish ends, which it would not tolerate; *fourthly*, Pakistan regard itself as a successor state to British India and has declared that its territory does not include any part of the Afghan territory, hence would not par with any of its own territory.[62]

To explain first point the Pakistan government authorities claim that the Afghan government leaders changed their view according to the situation and there has been difference in their assertions. Pakistan's Minister of Defence and Foreign Affairs said that Afghanistan government changed their ideas several times.[63]

> The Afghan claims have become stronger and more strident when there is a weak government in Pakistan. When Pakistan has a strong and stable government, Afghanistan's claims have become vague and less insistent.[64]

I.H. Baqai, a Pakistani writer express the difference in views made by Afghan government as sometime it indicated to the entire NWFP and the other areas and the region west of Indus river.[65] Pakistan government stated that the political recognition of this supposed area also stayed unclear, sometime as part of and United to Afghanistan, another time as autonomous region with the territory of Pakistan and the third as independent and the Pakistani government asserted the uncertainty is because of Afghanistan undecided thoughts.[66]

Sardar Wali Khan, the Afghan Ambassador in a reception set for him in Karachi explained the Afghan government stand and said:

> Our King has clearly stated and I as representative of Afghanistan with full sense of responsibility declared that Afghanistan has no claim on the territory and even if there were any, they have been given up in favour of Pakistan. Anything contrary to this, which may have appeared in the press in the past or may appear in the future should not be given credence at all and should be considered just a canard.[67]

However, Pakistan government expressed concern in Afghanistan's difference of opinion and called it not for welfare of Pakhtoons but Afghan leader's plan to bring all Pakhtoons under one united Afghan flag. The Afghan nationalist also asserted Baluchistan that is mostly by non-Pakhtoon tribes. Pakistan government claimed that through such scheme Afghanistan wants to have access to Arabian Sea.[68] So based on the Pakistani government remarks the Afghan government was not honest for what she claims the welfare of Pakhtoons but Pakhtoons are more utilised and instrumental for her plans and Pakistan called Afghanistan such stance as 'contradictory and ridiculous.' A Pakistani Ministry of Foreign Affairs spokesman said on one side the Afghan government is interfering in internal affairs of Afghanistan and on the other side she is the member of non-Alignment movement which the movement mainly talks about the non-interference in countries domestic affairs and respect for national sovereignty and territorial integrity and called Afghan stance as sincerity.[69] Pakistan government also stated that NEFP has never been part of any political entity of Afghanistan. Also the British Simon Commission stated that NWFP was not only the border of India but 'an international frontier of the first importance from the military point of view for the whole empire.'[70] So Pakistan argues as NWFP was part of the British India, it turn into its territory under the provision of the Indian Independence

Act of 1947, Section 7(1). So Pakistan as inheritor state took the area control after the Pakhtoons had executed "Instrument of Accession" in support of Pakistan.[71] Pakistan also rejected the right to self-determination asked by Afghanistan various government to be given to NWFP as it was before part of Pakistan.

Pakistan also argued that there was no such state before Ahmad Shah founded the Afghan Kingdom in 1747 and the areas were divided between the Safavi Empire of Iran and the Mughal Empire of India and the north-west India just for 50 years was part of Afghanistan which later the control has been given to the Sikhs and by them to the British.[72] It was argued by the Pakistan President Ayub Khan that if territorial expansion and reversion was based on the short period of 150 years then the world map[73] have been changed and said:

> All this concern for the Pathans in Pakistan was based on the claim that at one time in history Afghanistan held sway over some part of what is now West Pakistan. But there were also times of much longer duration that Delhi's sovereignty extended up to Kabul and beyond. If old conquest were to be our guide, then Pakistan should have more interest in the future of Pathans living in Afghanistan.[74]

Afghanistan historical assertion were rejected by Pakistan effectively and quite strongly on the basis that the trans-Indus tracts had been ceded to Nadir Shah and appropriated by Ahmad Shah only by virtue of force and remained a part of Afghanistan for a short period. Pakistan also affirmed that the Pakhtoons never formed together a nation and to maintain their unity they had made tribes. Also Pakistan said that while Afghanistan does not accept Pakhtoon on their side they will be divided into two independent states.[75] Pakistan also said that there were more Pashto speaking people in Pakistan than Afghanistan. She also said Afghanistan is multi-ethnic society consisting of Pakhtoons just comprise more than one in half of

Afghanistan population the remaining are Hazara, Turks, Uzbeks and Turkmens so if the same situation of Pakistan and Pakhtoonistan to be applied on Afghanistan she will lose its territories to her neighbours.[76] The Pakistan government also in a white paper said that it was the matter of ethnicity to determine the border of countries it would also result in disintegration of Afghanistan.[77] Pakistan government such argument demonstrates that it is also combined state and its Muslim citizens had accepted democratic and federal government.[78]

Pakistan also said Pakhtoonistan issue is just propaganda to pursue its expansionist policy.[79] The Pakistan government also said if the Afghan government was sincere to solve the Pakhtoonistan problem it should give the right to self-determination for the Pakhtoon inhabitants on both sides of Durand Line. According to the Foreign Minister of Pakistan, Manzur Qadir in 1960 while proposed the plebiscite to be conducted on both sides of Frontier, Mohammad Naim Afghan Foreign Minister expressed unwillingness.[80] Pakistan even went further in the issue and argued since the Pakhtoons living in Pakistan have expressed their interest being with Pakistan so it should also be asked from the Pakhtoons in Afghanistan, are they interested to be in Afghanistan or will join their Pakhtoon borders in Pakistan and according to the Pakistan Government hopefully they will vote for Pakistan rather than Afghanistan.[81] The Pakistan government also stated as two third of Pakhtoons are living in Pakistan it's more appropriate that the remaining should also join Pakhtoons in Pakistan as minority join with majority.

In addition a strong statement was made by Pakistan government against a sovereign Pakhtoonistan that it would not survive as its not the language, culture or race to support a state. A Pakistani writer said:

> Pakhtoonistan, it comes into being, will be an economic absurdity because...it will be composed of areas which

> are barren rocky and sparsely populated...Pakhtoonistan cannot survive for a day as an independent entity.[82]

Finally, Pakistan believes that Pakhtoonistan issue had roots in the domestic problem in Afghanistan confronted by the Afghan government and it was not based on logical and rational principles and the Afghan government had implemented such policy to turn away people mention from the crisis and backwardness of the country. According to Pakistan it was also used for world publicity.[83]

To conclude, Pakistan recognises the Durand Line as international boundary between the two neighbours left by British. She views Afghanistan assertion on Pakhtoonistan as sign of Afghan's emotions, domestic and geo-political force and expresses no readiness for talks on the issue. It also rejected Afghanistan's demand for Pakhtoonistan on historical, legal, pragmatic and economic bases. It furthermore claims that Afghanistan has no right to represent the Pakhtoons on Pakistan side of Durand Line and condemns it as interference in its internal issues.

Pashtu Perspective

To find a peaceful and pragmatic solution to the issue of Pakhtoonistan, Pakhtoon leaders' views gains significant role and they should be taken into confidence before taking any decision on the issue. The main obstacle is lack of communication and contact with tribal areas. Pakhtoon's observation and points are misinterpreted and presented by Afghan and Pakistan government for their government interest. So it makes it very difficult to come to a conclusion on Pakhtoon position.

Lord Curzon wrote that "no man who has never read a page of Indian history will prophesy about the frontier."[84] The point raised by Curzon seems to be valid still today. It's said that Curzon was the first to attempt in creating a common Pakhtoon awareness while demarcating the Frontier as province in 1901. Since that the Pakhtoon nationalism strengthened under the guidance of the Frontier Gandhi Abdul Ghafar Khan and his brother Khan Sahib. They established Khudai Khidmatgar to create a new and independent motherland for the Pakhtoons and when during the partition they were presented with limited choice either to join with Pakistan or India that sparked protest among them. Abdul Ghafar Khan as leader and Chief spokesman of the organisation said:

> This limits our choice to two alternatives, neither of which we are prepared to accept. We cannot vote as we want to vote for a Pathan State...In these circumstances, I am convinced that we cannot associate ourselves with this referendum.[85]

However, his brother Khan Sahib amended his statement as there was no way for an independent Pakhtoonistan. He accepted the referendum and its verdict, although previously in 1946 he had said:

> The frontier people have never bothered themselves about sections and groups. They will have their independence and nobody can force them to join anyone. It is for the Frontier people to decide and if they decided by majority vote that they will not join any group, nobody can force them.[86]

He also wrote to Nehru on 2 July 1947 that the Frontier people never thought of being part of Afghanistan 'we have learnt for the first time that Afghan government have officially approached the Government of India. We have been placed in an unenviable position; naturally, Afghan government is taking advantage of it and exploiting the situation.'[87] He because of difference in his idea that Peshawar could absorb Kabul and not the other way around broke with his brother. It is also believed that a "Ten Line Treaty" was signed with seals and thumb prints of many tribal chiefs that stated:

> We proclaim that we are part of Pakistan and we promise that in case of need we will help Pakistan...The

> Government of Pakistan will continue the allowances and other benefits which we are now receiving. The internal management of our tribe will remain as before.[88]

The Pro-Pakistan played vital role for no independent Pakhtoonistan. American writer Josif in his book wrote that the Pakhtoons in Pakistan were given less support for the formation of Pakhtoonistan.[89] If Pakhtoons in Pakistan of tribal areas did not support Pakistan would face shortages in supplies, facilities and the most importantly the subsidy. But it is injustice to say Pakhtoons have not expressed willingness for an independent state and Pakhtoonistan. In a meeting held in Bannu a resolution was approved by the members of *Khudai Khidmatgar* and young Pakhtoon Jirgas of the Frontier province and *Subah Sarhad* on 27 June 1947 stated to establish an independent Pakhtoonistan on Islamic principles, equality, democracy, justice, and rule of law.[90]

The declaration of Pakhtoonistan National Assembly stated:

> 'In the Tira Branch of the National Assembly of Pakhtoonistan having formed the first nucleus of free and democratic Muslim government amidst the lofty mountains of Tira hope...this rising plant may in a short grow into sturdy fruitful tree.'[91] Based on the Afghan pro reports the Pakhtoon people of the Pakistan side of the Durand Line have never accepted the foreign dominance and resisted against Pakistan colonialism. An essential tribal elder Malik Hakim Sayed promised his supporters were fight for an independent Pakhtooonistan and called Pakistan expansionist as great source of threat to Pakhtoonistan.[92] Another well-known Pakhtoon tribal elder in an interview with Al-Fath also called for an independent Pakhtoonistan. After the dismissal of the provincial governments in Frontier and Baluchistan such feelings were strengthened. So the Pakistan government attitude towards the Pakhtoons made them to upraise for their rights and for rights Pakhtoonistan independence.

B. Bizenjo, K.B. Marri, A.K. Bugti and Khan Wali Khan were the leaders who got saddened because their requirement and suggestion were not taken into consideration by the Pakistan government and asked their supporters to stand with them and fight for their political and economic rights.[93] There was difference in view of aforementioned leaders but all of them wanted autonomous Pakhtoonistan within the Pakistan territory. On the occasion of arrival of Abdul Ghaffar Khan in 1972, Maulana Mufti Mahmud said that Pakhtoonistan envisaged by Frontier Gandhi had been achieved, as the Pakhtoon had their own government.[94] Abdul Wali Khan supported that if Baluchistan and Frontier are part of Pakistan will benefit more than being independent.[95] The leader and father of the movement Khan Abdul Ghaffar Khan disproved the accusations against him that he had opposed the formation of Pakistan.[96] In an interview he was reported to have said that Pakhtoonistan is a secessionist term he said:

> This is no issue at all. It is only a demand to rename the area inhabited by Pakhtoons. But the vested interests deliberately distorted our position to give us a bad name. This has become a cliché to vilify our people, well, let there be any other name of identity the area inhabited by the Pakhtoons.[97]

Khan Abdul Ghaffar Khan made clear his point he just wanted and autonomous Pathan province to preserve the culture, language and the identity of Pakhtoons not for a separate state. Wali Khan asserted he did not believe on separation of any province from Pakistan and integration of Pakistan and he called his stand for the demographic right of the province was...ording to the constitution and not a crime and said:

> By "Pakhtoonistan" my father (Khan Abdul Ghaffar Khan) had always mean the existing province of NWFP which was to be renamed after the Pakhtoons. I myself and my Party, however, have never even used that expression.[98]

The statements and remarks made by the Pakhtoon leaders demonstrate that were not in favour of separation from Pakistan, they wanted autonomy to protect their identity, culture and language. The Pakistan government for its own stability and integrity should accept the proposal and political aspirations of Pakhtoon Leaders. Ignoring the Pakhtoons and keeping them away from their political and economic rights of their exploitation would also present an opening to Afghanistan to move up the issue.

References

1. M.A. Chaudhri, "The Relations of Pakistan with Afghanistan," Pakistan Horizon, Vol. Viii, No. 04, December 1955, p. 495.
2. Afghanistan News, Vol. IV, No. 40, December 1960, p. 18 and Vol. V, No. 53, January 1962, p. 09.
3. Rahaman Pazhwak, Pakhtoonistan: The Khyber Pass as the Focus of the New State of Pakhtunistan (London, n.p., n.d.), p. 10.
4. Khan Ghazi Kabuli, the President of Pakhtoon Jirga-i-Hind, in a personal unstructured interview New Delhi, 20 June 1981.
5. J.W. Spain, The Pathan Borderland (The Hauge, Mouton and Co., 1963), p. 40.
6. Supra, pp. 28-30.
7. Afghanistan News, Vol. IV, No. 48, August 1961, p. 05 also see A/PV. 2060, 10 October 1972, p. 02.
8. The Times, 30 April 1974.
9. UN/Doc., A/PV. 1692, 10 October 1968, pp. 15-16.
10. UN Doc., A/PV., 1692, 11 October 1968, p. 27.
11. *Ibid.*
12. UN/DOC., A/PV. 92, 30 September 1947, p. 314.
13. Louis Dupree, Pushtunistan, Vol. V, No. 2, November 1961, p. 04.
14. "Dr Najibullah Khan's statement on Pakhtoonistan Day," Afghanistan, Vol. VIII, No. 03, July-September 1953, p. 45.
15. UN/Doc., A/PV. 1690, 10 October 1968, p.16 and A/PV. 1701, 21 October 1968, p. 18.
16. Pakistan Times, 02 September 1954.
17. Surendra Chopra, no. 07, No. 47, pp. 314-315.
18. Asian Recorder, Vol. 01, No. 47, 19-25 November 1955, 521.
19. Rahman Pazhwak, no. 04, p. 59.

20. Pakistan Horizon, Vol. XXI, No.04, 1968, p. 379 and Pakistan Times, 24 December 1968.
21. Northern India Patrika, 20 January 1969.
22. Christian Science Monitor, 13 January 1969.
23. 'Conflict in Pakhtunistan,' n. 16, p. 12. UN Doc. A/PV. 1961, 11 October 1971, p. 09.
24. UN documents. A/PV. 1770, 29 September 1969, p. 04 and the Guardian, 7 June 1976.
25. Kabul Times, 19 December 1973, the Hindustan Times, 30 July 1973 and The Times, 27 July 1973.
26. The Times of India, 15 January 1974.
    Kabul Times, 16 June 1974.
27. Kabul Times, 29 June 1974.
28. The Patriot, 27 January 1974.
    The Times, 18 October 1974.
29. UN Doc., A/PV. 2265, 10 October 1974, pp. 91-92.
30. The Times of India, 27 September 1974. Asian Recorder, Vol. XXI, No. 06, 5-11, February 1975, p. 12406.
31. *Ibid.,* Vol. XXI, No. 04, 22-28 January 1975, p. 12406.
32. Kabul Times, 04 November 1975.
33. The Tribune, 08 April 1976.
34. UN Do., A/PV 2359, 24 September 1975, pp. 59-60.
35. The Patriot, 19 July 1977.
36. The Statesman, 13 October 1977.
37. UN Doc., A/S 10/PV. 19, 06 June 1978, pp. 23-25.
38. Asian Recorder, Vol. XXIV, No. 46. 12-18, November 1978, p. 14601.
39. The Times of India, 11 February 1979.
    Kabul Times, 04 July 1979.
40. Rajendra Sareen, n. 58.
41. The Muslim, 21 September 1979.
    Indian Express, 25 September 1979.
42. The Times, 30 April 1979.
43. Middle East Journal, Vol. VI, Winter 1952, p. 58.
44. K Warikoo, Afghanistan Challenges and Opportunities, New Delhi, Pentagon Press, 2007, pp. 130-131.
45. Tehran Times, September 21, 2008.
46. http://www.rferl.org/content/Article/1075982.html.

47. UN/Doc., A/PV. 2263,09 October 1974, pp. 112-117.
48. S.M. Qureshi, "The Frontier Dispute between Afghanistan and Pakistan," Pacific Affairs, Vol. XXXIX, Nos 1 and 2, Spring-Summer, 1966, p. 103.
49. S.M. Burke, Pakistan's Foreign Policy (London, Oxford University Press, 1973), p. 85.
50. Its correct that the British mission led by Durand had gone unarmed unlike the previous mission led by Lord Roberts, whom the Amir had refused to receive. But it is not that the British mission had gone at the instance of Amir Abdur Rahman, rather he had delayed the matter for years to be settled since he was suspicious of the British intension.

    For Dept. Sec. F Progs., Nos. 67-91, N.A.I., April 1893, No. 68.
51. For Dept. Sec. F Progs., Nos. 71-158, N.A.I., December 1893, No. 154.
52. Sir Percy Sykes, Sir Mortimer Duran: A Biography (London, Macmillan, 1926), p. 103.
53. C.U. Aitcheson, A Collection of Treaties, Engagements and Sanads in Relation to India and Neighbouring Countries (Calcutta, Government of India Central Publication Branch, 1933,Reprint 1973), Vol. XII, part II, pp. 256-257.

    Dept. Sec. F Progs., Nos. 159-199, N.A.I. December 1983, No. 183.
54. Pakistan Horizon, Vol. XVI, n.03, 1963, p. 263.
55. UN Doc., A/PV. 1690, 10 October 1968, p. 15.
56. Pakistan, National Assembly Debates, Vol. V, No. 30, 18 July 1974, p. 217.
57. UN Doc., A/PV. 2263, 9 October, 1974 pp. 113-115.
58. M.A. Chaudhri, n. 01, p. 496.
59. Pakistan Times, 30 December 1949.
60. Manchester Guardian, 2 February 1951.

    Pakistan Times, 22 May 1974.
61. Pakistan, Constituent Assembly Debates, Vol. II, 09 January 1950, p. 378.
62. UN Doc., A/PV. 2263, 9 October 1974, p. 112.

    President Ayub Khan regarded Pakhtoonistan issue as an artificial one devised that the Afghan leaders for their Selfish motives and that had impaired the relations between the two countries. The Times, 13 July 1961.
63. Pakistan National Assembly Debates Vol. V, No. 30, 18 July 1974, pp. 240-241.

64. Mohammad Ayub Khan, Friends not Masters: A Political Autobiography, Lahore, Oxford University Press, 1967, p. 176.
65. I.H. Baqai, "Relations between Afghanistan and Pakistan," Pakistan Horizon, Vol. 1, No. 03, September 1948, p. 213.
66. Conflict in Pashtunistan, n. 86.
67. Policy at Kabul, 23 June 1948.
68. Feroz Ahmad, n. 94, p. 86.
69. Foreign Affairs, Pakistan, Vol. 01, No. 03, August 1974, p. 27.

    Aziz Ahmed, Pakistan's Minister of State for Defence and Foreign Affairs, criticised Afghanistan policy and pointed out that Pakistan had been putting up with Afghan interference for more than one-fourth of century, which had been 'blatant, shameless and provocative,' but which would not be tolerated further. Pakistan, National Assembly Debates, Vol. V, No.03, 18 July 1974, p. 240.
70. Cited in Sir William Barton, India's North West Frontier (London, Murray, 1939), p. 05.
71. Though Pakistan regarded itself a successor of British Empire in India, it is significant that regarding the question of UN membership, India was considered a successor state and Pakistan had to apply for new membership.
72. Zubeida Hasan, 'The Foreign Policy of Afghanistan,' Pakistan Horizon, Vol. XVII, No. 01, 1964, pp. 55-56.
73. J.R.V. Prescott, n.9, p. 92.
74. Mohammad Ayub Khan, n. 64, p. 176.
75. S.M. Burke, n. 48, pp. 87-88.
76. Pakistan Times, 2 November 1974.
77. White Paper, dated to September 1961, pp. 05-07.

    Dawn, 4 September 1961, Minister of External Affairs, Government of Pakistan.
78. 'Conflict in Pakhtunistan,' n. 16, p. 14.
79. Politicus, 'Playing with Fire,' Pakistan Times, 22 May 1974.
80. S.M.M. Qureshi, n. 48, p. 110.
81. Un Doc., A/PV., 1698, 16 October, pp. 20-21.
82. M.A. Chaudhri, n. 01, pp. 496-497.
83. Hafeez R, Khan, "Afghanistan and Pakistan," p. 58.
84. Cited in J.W. Spain, "Pakistan North West Frontier," Middle East Journal, Vol. VIII, Winter 1954, p. 39.
85. Cited in J.W. Spain, "Pakistan North West Frontier," Middle East Journal, Vol. VIII, winter 1954, p. 39.

86. Cited in Rahman Pazhwak, No. 04, p. 110.
87. Pyare Lal, Mahatma Gandhi-The Last Phase (Allahabad, Navajevan, 1956), p. 281.
88. New York Times, 23 May 1949.
89. Harold G. Joseph, Political Stability on the North West Frontier of South Asia, (Washington, Foreign Service Institute, Department of State, 1951), p. 26.
90. Appendix 5.
91. Cited in Dorothea Seelye Franck, n. 73, p. 59.
92. Prize Winning Book Banned in Pakhtunistan, Afghan News, Vol. V, No. 35, June 1960, p. 22.
93. Shirin Tahir-Kheli "The Foreign Policy of New Pakistan," Orbis, Vol. XX, No. 03, Fall 1976, p. 747.
94. "Seven Baluchis Martyred," Afghanistan News, Vol. IV, No. 37, September 1960, p. 22.
95. Sayed Yousuf Raza, "Pak Young Turks threaten Action," The Tribune, 26 January 1979.
96. Satish Kumar, n.39, pp. 29-30.
97. Times of India and the Tribune, 14 October 1977.
98. The Tribune, 19 October 1977.

CHAPTER-V

CONCLUSION

Afghanistan and Pakistan argument on the Pakhtoonistan issue has its roots in history. The neighbouring Afghanistan never accepted the Durand Line defined and demarcated by the British in 1893 as it divided the Pakhtoons from both side of the border. But the Pakistani government have recognised the agreement and the Durand Line as international border between the both neighbours of Afghanistan and Pakistan. Afghans discontent caused for the conception of Pakhtoonistan and the request for self-determination.

Due to the oppressive policies and strategies adopted by the Pakistan government on the Pakhtoons the Afghan governments stand has changed from time to time as before they were asking for an autonomous Pakhtoon region but now for an independent Pakhtoonistan state. The Afghan nation have expressed their support for the Pakhtoons on the other side of the border because of the ethnicity and similarities existed among them and also that the Durand Line was imposed on Afghan Amir as he was under pressure to sign the agreement and the Afghan government called it as unfair treaty.

The Afghan demand has never been clearly demonstrate because of the situation and crisis in the country as it was more objective. The question of ethnic affinity has been confused with the legality of the Durand Line, which made the Afghan claims rather weak. Moreover, if Afghans do not recognise the reality of the Durand Line and seek a re-demarcation of their frontier with Pakistan, it means, despite their denial of such intentions, they have an eye on some Pakistani territory. This purpose was more tangible when the Afghan government expressed interest to have access to the Arabian Sea as the country is landlocked. It's also believed based on facts and data's published that Amir Abdur Rahman was under immense internal and external pressure. Furthermore, Afghanistan never neglected the issue of Pakhtoons and Pakhtoonistan. The Afghan leaders in international summits have raised their voice and concern for the issue of Pakhtoonistan and the right of Pakhtoons for right to self-determination.

It was the referendum of 1947 in Pakistan that declined Pakistan argument. The referendum held in a way that the tribal areas and the princely states were ignored just the settled areas was the area for referendum. So only 5,72, 788 people out of 40 lakh[1] population were entitled to caste, that after the voting process Pakistan got 2,89,244 votes in its favour about 50 per cent of the total votes and India only 2,874. The remaining boycotted the referendum on the request of *Khudai Khidmatgaar* Movement leader and the Congress.

Comparatively the votes casted in the referendum were less by 83,871 votes than the number of votes of 1946 general election.[2] So about the people of princely states and tribal people of 25 lakh didn't cast their votes. The Pakistan government ignored those areas because of no presence of government representative. But the argument is fragile because referendum requires no legislative assembly.

Also, Pakistan government assertion that the tribal Jirgas had also supported the government was not credible because they were under the control of British representatives operating under the government of Pakistan. So there is no legitimate data that the tribal people had accepted the political change, furthermore, the Pakhtoons based on the right to self-determination were to be presented with choices weather to join India, Pakistan or Afghanistan or to become an independent state.

This is the fact that Pakhtoons consider they are separate from Pakistan and close to Afghanistan, then have been deprived of their right to self-determination because of the referendum. Khan Abdul Ghaffar Khan the leader and the chairman of the *Khudai Khidmatgaar* government also validated this. In fact, most of the borders in Asia have been demarcated by colonial and Imperialist European governments for the protection of their national interests and that is complicated to recognise or admit the geniuses and purity of these borders.

Afghanistan had criticised against the British but to gain negotiate on the issue will create problems between the two independent states of Pakistan and Afghanistan and would influence their national sovereignty and territorial integrity. Also it would be inappropriate to move up the issue of legality of the boundaries that has been there since a long time.

Afghanistan and Pakistan have lived together 68 years with strained and complex relations. If Pakistani leaders and rulers provide the right to self-determination to Pakhtoons and their other economic and political rights preserved and if they were treated as equal citizens of Pakistan in terms of welfare and development they could have win the hearts and mind of the Afghan rulers.

It was Pakhtoons' civil and political right to rise against the inequality and the Punjabi dominance in Pakistan political system where they were treated as superior and the Pakhtoons as inferior in many aspect and dimension and to call for their autonomy and their right to participate in decision and national policy making process.

However, no government in Pakistan supported and expressed willingness for the issue and moreover suppressed the Pakhtoons because to deprived them from the political space and power. If the Pakistan government express readiness in providing a free port based on the request of the Afghan government at Karachi or Baluchistan so Afghanistan can have access to the Arabian Sea it can lay a significant rôle in development and expansion of friendly and cordial relations between two nations.

Thus, its seen that it is not possible or acceptable for Pakistan to provide a free port for Afghanistan but the establishment of open transit system would be probable. So the step would not only help in strengthening of bilateral relations between Afghanistan and Pakistan but also effective for both from economic perspective.[3]

Besides the disagreements from both neighbouring countries the superpower factor is also playing major role in relations between them as both superpowers are worried of Pakhtoonistan area to be used by them against each other. It's because of such rivalries of superpowers that the region confronted with multiple regional and international challenges.

We can say it is more the result of superpower reactions that the area and the region have been facing tension with serious security threats. Hostilities between Afghanistan and Pakistan started as a result of historic forces of ethnic regionalism acquired the form of Pakhtoonistan demand. It was while the United States was trying to contain communism in South, South-East and South-West Asia. Alignment with one bloc or the other was very common during fifties. The Superpower took the benefit of political instability, regional conflict and backwardness and for the protection of their interest utilised them.

However, the Soviet invasion of Afghanistan totally changed the nature of superpowers involvement in the region. Afghanistan's elite alleged United States, China, Saudi Arabia and other Muslim countries military and economic assistance to defeat Russian Red Army and contain communism threat to the security of Afghanistan. Also the

Soviet Army presence in Afghanistan and the refugees to originated to the neighbouring Pakistan States of Baluchistan and Frontier accelerated momentum of rebel's movement in that country.

Pakistani elites called it as threat to the security and national interest of Pakistan. So the superpower involvement has been a factor for strained of relations between Afghanistan and Pakistan beside the other causes. The West viewed that the Soviet invasion of Afghanistan is the Tsarist purpose to have access to the Indian Ocean and warm waters and to create their power in the region but the long-term presence of the Soviet forces cannot be condoned.

Several Soviet comment seem to imply that the primary Soviet object is to prevent Afghanistan from becoming a hostile base rather than to retain the country as a strategic ally or base for spreading Communist ideology. But the presence of military personal in Afghanistan is providing the US and China with an alibi to go ahead with their plans to establish their large scale presence in the strategic South-West Asia and the Indian Ocean Region.

Previously, the Soviet aim to countenance the US influence in close proximity to her tender under-belly, is not being promoted in any way by the presence of Soviet military in Afghanistan. The need is to improve the international environment by political diplomacy which could facilitate an amicable settlement of the Afghan crisis.

The guarantee of non-interference in the Afghan affairs by all outside powers seems to be the cornerstone of any political solution of the Afghan crisis. A genuine non-aligned Afghanistan should be a better guardian of Soviet interests, since in past Afghans had respected the Soviet responsibility concerning security. This in turn would help reduce fear and tension between Pakistan and Afghanistan and improve their bilateral relations.

The desirability of better relationship between the two neighbours cannot be underestimated. The rising tension prevents the outside powers from interfering in this area. In fact, the normalisation of relations between the two countries is essential not only for maintaining peace in the region but also for domestic stability and development of both these countries. With the approved relations, both the countries can have joint ventures like hydro-electric projects and steel mills to make use of their resources for mutual benefit and help to solve their socio-economic difficulties.

However, the normalisation of relations depends on a number of factors. First, the political developments in both the countries will have a profound impact on their bilateral relations. If political instability continues, the external powers would seize the opportunities to destabilise the region and gain hegemony over the area. For instance, if Pakhtoon and Baluchi leadership, which does not feel integrated into the national mainstream of Pakistan, is taken over by the militant hard-liners and the Pakistani elite ignore their genuine aspirations, the ensuing situation will present an opportunity to Kabul to fulfil her objective of gaining an access to the Arabian Sea. Moscow too might be tempted to support the Baluch and Pakhtoon liberation movement as the success of any such movement should give it an access to the Indian Ocean without directly encroaching upon the territorial integrity and sovereignty of Pakistan.

Secondly, the equation Pakistan keeps with the superpowers will also determine the nature of its ties with Kabul, if Islamabad ceases to act on behalf of one superpower at the cost of the other; it should help here to evolve a working relationship with both. This will have a healthier effect on their relations with Kabul. Thirdly, the normalisation of relations will depend on the capability of the national leaders to ensure domestic support to their policies in their respective countries. The capability of leaders in this regard can jeopardise not only the process of detente but also endanger their lines. Daud's softened attitude towards Pakistan in the later years of his rule seems to have been of the major factor for his murder and the overthrow of his regime.

Lastly, the element of flexibility and accommodation in their approach to the major issue like Pakhtoonistan and the Afghan crisis would influence and determine their bilateral relations. This desirability for peace of the region and world at large that both the countries make sincere efforts to normalise their relations through bilateral negotiations while keeping their emotions and narrow national interests for aside.

References

1. According to 1941 census of India, the last held before the partition of the Country, North West Frontier Province (District and Trans-frontier Posts) had 3,084,334 population. Assuming 2.5 per cent average population in 1947.

   I.D. Scott, Census of India 1941: North West Frontier Province (Delhi, Government of India), 1942, Vol. X.
2. Britannica Book of the Year, 1950 (London, Knight and Forster, 1953), p. 488.
3. For substantiation of this view see Surendra Chopra, "Indo-Pakistan Relations: A Study of New Challenge and opportunities," in Surendra Chopra, ed., Studies in India's Foreign Policy (Amritsar, Gurunank Dev University, 1983), pp. 203-204.

Appendix-I
Durand Line Agreement
November 12, 1893

Agreement between Amir Abdur Rahman Khan, GCSI, and Sir Henry Mortimer Durand, KCIE, CSI.

Whereas certain questions have arisen regarding the frontier of Afghanistan on the side of India, and whereas both His Highness the Amir and the Government of India are desirous of settling these questions by friendly understanding, and of fixing the limit of their respective spheres of influence, so that for the future there may be no difference of opinion on the subject between the allied governments, it is hereby agreed as follows:

1. The eastern and southern frontier of his Highness's dominions, from Wakhan to the Persian border, shall follow the line shown in the map attached to this agreement.
2. The Government of India will at no time exercise interference in the territories lying beyond this line on the side of Afghanistan, and His Highness the Amir will at no time exercise interference in the territories lying beyond this line on the side of India.
3. The British Government thus agrees to His Highness the Amir retaining Asmar and the valley above it, as far as Chanak. His Highness agrees, on the other

hand, that he will at no time exercise interference in Swat, Bajaur, or Chitral, including the Arnawai or Bashgal valley. The British Government also agrees to leave to His Highness the Birmal tract as shown in the detailed map already given to his Highness, who relinquishes his claim to the rest of the Waziri country and Dawar. His Highness also relinquishes his claim to Chageh.

4. The frontier line will hereafter be laid down in detail and demarcated, wherever this may be practicable and desirable, by joint British and Afghan commissioners, whose object will be to arrive by mutual understanding at a boundary which shall adhere with the greatest possible exactness to the line shown in the map attached to this agreement, having due regard to the existing local rights of villages adjoining the frontier.

5. With reference to the question of Chaman, the Amir withdraws his objection to the new British cantonment and concedes to the British Government the rights purchased by him in the Sirkai Tilerai water. At this part of the frontier the line will be drawn as follows:

   From the crest of the Khwaja Amran range near the Psha Kotal, which remains in British territory, the line will run in such a direction as to leave Murgha Chaman and the Sharobo spring to Afghanistan, and to pass half-way between the New Chaman Fort and the Afghan outpost known locally as Lashkar Dand. The line will then pass half-way between the railway station and the hill known as the Mian Baldak, and, turning southwards, will rejoin the Khwaja Amran range, leaving the Gwasha Post in British territory, and the road to Shorawak to the west and south of Gwasha in Afghanistan. The British Government will not exercise any interference within half a mile of the road.

6. The above articles of' agreement are regarded by the Government of India and His Highness the Amir of Afghanistan as a full and satisfactory settlement of all the principal differences of opinion which have arisen between them in regard to the frontier; and both the Government of India and His Highness the Amir undertake that any differences of detail, such as those which will have to be considered hereafter by the officers appointed to demarcate the boundary line, shall be settled in a friendly spirit, so as to remove for the future as far as possible all causes of doubt and misunderstanding between the two governments.
7. Being fully satisfied of His Highness's goodwill to the British Government, and wishing to see Afghanistan independent and strong, the Government of India will raise no objection to the purchase and import by His Highness of munitions of war, and they will themselves grant him some help in this respect. Further, in order to mark their sense of the friendly spirit in which His Highness the Amir has entered into these negotiations, the Government of India undertake to increase by the sum of six lakhs of rupees a year the subsidy of twelve lakhs now granted to His Highness.

H. M. Durand,
Amir Abdur Rahman Khan.
Kabul, November 12, 1893.

APPENDIX II

Treaty with Amir Habibullah continuing the agreement which had existed between the British Government and Amir Abdur Rahman Khan 1905

His Majesty Siraj-ul-Milat-waud-din Amir Habibullah Khan, Independent King of state of Afghanistan and its dependencies, on the one part, and the Honourable Mr. Louis William Dane, Foreign Secretary of the Mighty Government of India and Representative of the Exalted British Government on the other part.

His side Majesty hereby agree to this that, in the principles and in the matters of subsidiary importance of the treaty regarding internal and external affairs and of the engagement which His Highness, my late father, that is, Zia-ul-milat-wa-ud-din, who has found mercy, may God enlighten his tomb concluded and acted upon with the exalted British Government, I also have acted, am acting and will act up on the same agreement and compact, and I will not contravene them in any dealing or in any promise.

The said Honourable Mr. Louis William Dane does hereby agree to this that as to the very agreement and engagement which the Exalted British Government concluded and acted upon with the noble father of his majesty Siraj-ul-milat-wa-ud-din, that is, His Highness Zialul-milat-wa-ud-din, who has found mercy, regarding the internal and external affairs and matters of principle of subsidiary importance, I confirm them and write that they (the British

Government) will not act contrary to those agreements and engagement in any way or at any time.

Made on Tuesday the 14th day of Muharram-ul-Flaram of the year 1323 Hijri, corresponding to the 21st day of March of the Year 1905 A.D.

(Persian Seal of Amir Habibullah Khan)
Amir Habibullah
Louis W, Dane
Foreign Secretary representing Govt. of India

APPENDIX III

Treaty of Peace between the illustrious British Government and the Independent Afghan Government concluded at Rawalpindi on the 8th August 1919, corresponding to 11th Zirada, 1337 Hijra.

The following Article for the restoration of peace has been agreed upon by the British government and the Afghan government:

Article 1

From the date of the signing of this treaty there shall be peace between the British Government, in the one part, and the Government of Afghanistan on the other.

Article 2

In view of the circumstances which have brought about the present war between the British government and Government of Afghanistan, the British Government, to mark their displeasure, withdraw the privileged enjoyed by former Amirs of importing arms, ammunition or warlike munitions through India to Afghanistan.

Article 3

The arrears of the late Amir's subsidy are furthermore confiscated, and so subsidy is granted to the present Amir.

Article 4

At the same time, the British Government are desirous of the re-establishment of the old friendship that has so long existed between Afghanistan and Great Britain, provided they have guarantees that the Afghan government. The British Government are prepared, therefore provided the Afghan Government prove this by their acts and conduct, to receive another Afghan mission after six months for the discussion and settlement of matters of common interest to the two governments and the re-establishment of the old friendship on a satisfactory basis.

Article 5

The Afghan Government accepts the Indo-Afghan frontier accepted but the late Amir. They further agree to the early demarcation by a British Commission of the un-demarcated portion of the line west of Khyber where the recent Afghan aggression took place, and to accept such boundary as the British Commission may lay down. The British troops on this side will remain in their present position until such demarcation has been effected.

Ali Ahmad Khan
Commissary for Home Affairs
And Chief of the Peace Delegation
The Afghan Government

A.H. Grant
Foreign Secretary to the
Government of India and of
Chief of the Peace Delegation
of British Government

APPENDIX IV

Whereas the following territories, that is to say the districts of Peshawar, Kohat and Hazara (as altered by the Notification of the Punjab Government No. 994, dated the 17th October, 1901) the Bannu and Marwat Tehsils of the district of Bannu and the Tank, Dera Ismail Khan and Kulachi Tehsils of the district of Dera Ismail Khan (as altered by the notification of Punjab Government No. 993, dated the 17th October 1901) are part of the dominions of his majesty the King, emperor of India; and whereas it is expedient that the said territories, which are not under the administration of the Lieutenant Governor of the Punjab should be formed into a separate province and constitute a chief commissionership under the administration of a chief commissioner, know all men, and it is hereby proclaimed, that His Excellency, the Viceroy and Governor-General of India in Council, in exercise of the Powers conferred by Section 3 of the Government of India Act. 1854 (17 & 18 Vict, c. 77) and with the sanction and approbation of the Secretary of State for India, is pleased hereby to take the said territories under his immediate authority and management on and with effect from the ninth day of November, 1901, and further to direct that, on and with effect from the said ninth day of November 1901, he said territories shall be formed into a separate province and constituted a Chief Commissionership, to be called, the Chief Commissionership of the North West Frontier Province and to be administered by a chief commissioner.

By Orders of His Excellency the Viceroy
Governor-General of India in Council
J.P. NEWETT
Secretary to Government of India

پښتونستان

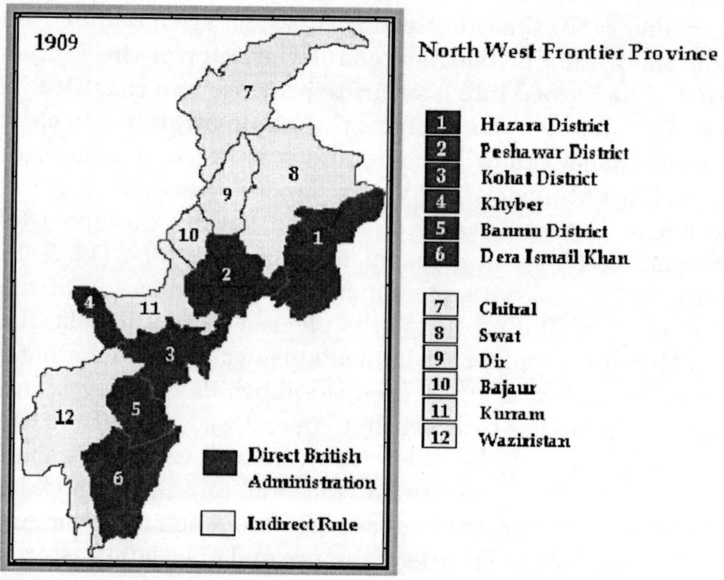
1909
North West Frontier Province
1 Hazara District
2 Peshawar District
3 Kohat District
4 Khyber
5 Bannu District
6 Dera Ismail Khan
7 Chitral
8 Swat
9 Dir
10 Bajaur
11 Kurram
12 Waziristan
Direct British Administration
Indirect Rule

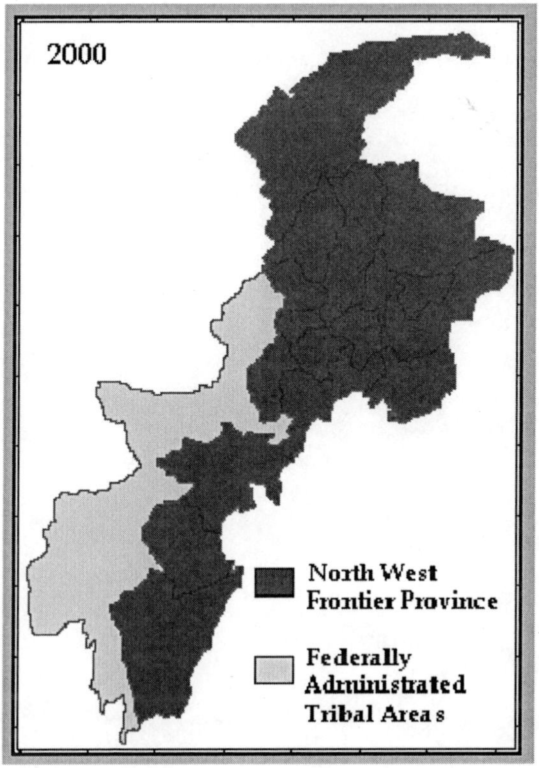
2000
North West
Frontier Province
Federally
Administrated
Tribal Areas

Appendix-V

Afghanistan-Union of Soviet Socialist Republics: Treaty of Friendship, Goodneighbourliness and Cooperation*

[Done at Moscow, December 5, 1978]

The Union of Soviet Socialist Republics

and

The Democratic Republic of Afghanistan,

Reaffirming their commitment to the aims and principles of the Soviet-Afghan Treaties of 1921 and 1931, which laid the basis for friendly and good neighbour relations between the Soviet and Afghan peoples and which meet their basic national interests,

Willing to strengthen in every way friendship and all-round cooperation between the two countries,

Being determined to develop social and economic achievements of the Soviet and Afghan peoples, to safeguard

---

* [Reprinted from the TASS English text of December 5, 1978, provided to International Legal Materials by the Embassy of the Union of Soviet Socialist Republics at Washington, D.C.]

[The Treaty came into force on May 27, 1979, with the exchange of instruments of ratification at Kabul.]

their security and independence, to come out resolutely for the cohesion of all the forces fighting for peace, national independence, democracy and social progress,

Expressing their firm determination to facilitate the strengthening of peace and security in Asia and the whole world, to make their contribution toward developing relations among states and strengthening fruitful and mutually beneficial cooperation in Asia, attaching great importance to the further consolidation of the contractual-legal basis of their relations,

Reaffirming their dedication to the aims and principles of the United Nations Charter,

Decided to conclude the present Treaty of Friendship, Goodneighbourliness and Cooperation and agreed on the following:

Article 1

The High Contracting Parties solemnly declare their determination to strengthen and deepen the inviolable friendship between the two countries and to develop all-round cooperation on the basis of equality, respect for national sovereignty, territorial integrity and non-interference in each other's internal affairs.

Article 2

The High Contracting Parties shall make efforts to strengthen and broaden mutually beneficial economic, scientific and technical cooperation between them. With these aims in view, they shall develop and deepen cooperation in the fields of industry, transport and communications, agriculture, the use of natural resources, development of the power-generating industry and other branches of economy, to give each other assistance in the training of national personnel and in planning the development of the national economy. The two sides shall expand trade on the basis of the principles of equality, mutual benefit, and most favoured nation treatment.

Article 3

The High Contracting Parties shall promote the development of cooperation and exchange of experience in the fields of science, culture, art, literature, education, health services, the press, radio, television, cinema, tourism, sport, and other fields.

The two sides shall facilitate the expansion of cooperation between organs of state power and public organisations, enterprises, cultural and scientific institutions with a view to making a deeper acquaintance of the life, work experience and achievements of the peoples of the two countries.

Article 4

The High Contracting Parties, acting in the spirit of the traditions of friendship and goodneighbourliness, as well as the UN Charter, shall consult each other and take by agreement appropriate measures to ensure the security, independence, and territorial integrity of the two countries.

In the interests of strengthening the defense capacity of the High Contracting Parties, they shall continue to develop cooperation in the military field on the basis of appropriate agreements concluded between them.

Article 5

The Union of Soviet Socialist Republics respects the policy of nonalignment which is pursued by the Democratic Republic of Afghanistan and which is an important factor for maintaining international peace and security.

The Democratic Republic of Afghanistan respects the policy of peace pursued by the Union of Soviet Socialist Republics and aimed at strengthening friendship and cooperation with all countries and peoples.

Article 6

Each of the High Contracting Parties solemnly declares that it shall not join any military or other alliances or take part in any groupings of states, as well as in actions or measures directed against the other High Contracting Party.

Article 7

The High Contracting Parties shall continue to make every effort to defend international peace and the security of the peoples, to deepen the process of relaxation of international tension, to spread it to all areas of the world, including Asia, to translate it into concrete forms of mutually beneficial cooperation among states and to settle international disputed issues by peaceful means.

The two sides shall actively contribute toward general and complete disarmament, including nuclear disarmament, under effective international control.

Article 8

The High Contracting Parties shall facilitate the development of cooperation among Asian states and the establishment of relations of peace, good neighbourliness and mutual confidence among them and the creation of an effective security system in Asia on the basis of joint efforts by all countries of the continent.

Article 9

The High Contracting Parties shall continue their consistent struggle against machinations by the forces of aggression, for the final elimination of colonialism and racism in all their forms and manifestations.

The two sides shall cooperate with each other and with other peace-loving states in supporting the just struggle of the peoples for their freedom, independence, sovereignty and social progress.

Article 10

The High Contracting Parties shall consult each other on all major international issues affecting the interests of the two countries.

Article 11

The High Contracting Parties state that their commitments under the existing international treaties do not contradict the provisions of the present treaty and undertake not to conclude any international agreements incompatible with it.

Article 12

Questions which may arise between the High Contracting Parties concerning the interpretation or application of any provision of the present treaty, shall be settled bilaterally, in the spirit of friendship, mutual understanding and respect.

Article 13

The present treaty shall remain in force within twenty years of the day it becomes effective. Unless one of the High Contracting Parties declares six months before the expiration of this term of its desire to terminate the treaty, it shall remain in force for the next five years until one of the High Contracting Parties warns in writing the other Party, six months before the expiration of current five-year term, about its intention to terminate the treaty.

Article 14

If one of the High Contracting Parties expresses the wish in the course of the twenty-year term of the treaty to terminate it before its expiration date, it shall notify in writing the other Party, six months before its suggested date of expiration of the treaty, about its desire to terminate the treaty before the expiration of the term and may consider the treaty terminated as of the date thus set.

Article 15

The present treaty shall be ratified and take effect on the day of exchange of the instruments of ratification, which is to take place in Kabul.

Done in duplicate, each in the Russian and Dari languages, both texts being equally authentic.

Done in Moscow on December 5, 1978.

For the Union of Soviet Socialist Republics
L. Brezhnev

For the Democratic Republic of Afghanistan
N. Mohammad Tarakki

Bibliography

1. A.Z. Hilali, "The Costs and Benefits of the Afghan War for Pakistan", *Contemporary South Asia,* Vol. 11, No. 3, 2002.
2. A.Z. Hilali, "The Soviet Penetration into Afghanistan and the Marxist Coup," *The Journal of Salavic Military Studies,* Vol. 18, issue 04, January 12, 2005.
3. A.Z. Hilali, *US – Pakistan Relationship: Soviet Invasion of Afghanistan* (Hants: Ashgate Publishing Limited, 2005).
4. Abdul Samad Ghaus, *The Fall of Afghanistan: An Insider's Account* (London: Brassey's International Defence Publishers, 1988).
5. Abdur Rahman, "The Life of Abdur Rahman Amir of Afghanistan," ed., Mir Munshi Sultan Mohammed Khan (London, Murray, 1990) Vol. II.
6. Afghanistan News, Vol. IV, No. 40, December 1960, p. 18 and Vol. V, No. 53, January 1962.
7. Afghanistan News, Vol. IV, No. 48, August 1961, p. 05.
8. Ahmad Rashir Malik, "Warming Ties with Russia", *Oriental Review.*
9. Ahmed Rashid, *Taliban: The Story of the Afghan Warlords* (London, Pan Books: 2001).
10. Ahmed Rashid, *The Taliban* (London: Yale University Press, 2001).

11. Aitchison Treaties, n. 10, p. 218. For the text of treaty see pp. 255-256.
12. Dept. Sec. F. Prog., Nos. 159-199. N.A.I., December 1893, No. 160.
13. Amin Saikal, *Modern Afghanistan: A History of Struggle and Survival* (New York: I. B. Tauris, 2004).
14. Anatol Lieven, *Pakistan: A Hard Country,* (London: Penguin Books, 2011).
15. Anatoly S. Chernyaev, *My Six Years with Gorbachev* (University Park: The Pennsylvania State University Press, 2000).
16. Anees Jillani, "Pak Afghan Relations: 1958 to 1988", *Pakistan Horizon,* Vol. 46, No. 1, (Karachi: January 1993).
17. Angelo Rasanayagam, *Afghanistan: A Modern History* (London and New York: I. B. Tauris, 2002).
18. Aparna Pande, *Explaining Pakistan's Foreign Policy: Escaping India,* (Oxon: Routledge Contemporary South Asia, 2011).
19. Arney George, *Afghanistan,* (London: Mandarin Paperbacks, 1990).
20. Arnold Fletcher, Afghanistan: Highway of Conquest (New York, Cornell University Press, 1965).
21. Hasan Kakar, "Afghanistan from Disintegration to reunification: 1880-1884," Afghanistan. Vol. XXIII, No. 1, 1970.
22. Barnett R. Rubin, "Soviet Lessons of Afghanistan Assure Pullout Will Go On", *Los Angeles Times,* November 14, 1988.
23. Bijan Omrani, "The Durand Line: History and Problems of the Afghan –Pakistan Border," *Asian Affairs*, Vol. XL, No. 11, (London: July 2009).
24. Britannica Book of the Year, 1950 (London, Knight and Forster, 1953).
25. C.U. Aitcheson, *A Collection of Treaties, Engagements and Sanads in Relation to India and Neighbouring*

Countries, (Calcutta, Government of India Central Publication Branch, 1933, Reprint, 1973), Vol. Xiii, part II.

26. C.U. Aitcheson, A Collection of Treaties, Engagements and Sanads in Relation to India and Neighbouring Countries (Calcutta, Government of India Central Publication Branch, 1933, Reprint 1973), Vol. XII, part II.
27. Darrel J. Bennett, Jr, "From the Carter to the Bush Doctrine: An In-Depth Analysis of US Middle Eastern Policy", Policy Analysis Paper, Centre for the Study of the Presidency and Congress (Washington: 2007), www.thepresidency.org/storage/documents/Calkins/Bennett.pdf
28. Daveed Garttenstein-Ross and Tara Vassefi, "The Forgotten History of Afghanistan-Pakistan Relations," *Yale Journal of International Affairs*, March 2012, *http://yalejournal.org/wp-content/uploads/2012/04/Article-Gartenstein_Ross-and-Vassefi.pdf*
29. Diego Cordovez and Selig S. Harrison, *Out of Afghanistan: The Inside story of the Soviet Withdrawal,* (New York : Oxford University Press, 1995).
30. Dilip Mukherjee, "Afghanistan under Daud: Relations with Neighbouring State", *Asian Survey,* Vol. 15, No. 4, (California: April 1975).
31. Dr Noor Shah, *Pak-Afghan Relations: In the Perspective of War on Terrorism".*
32. Edward Thompson and G.T. Garratt, Rise and Fulfilment of British Rule in India (London, Oxford University Press 1925).
33. Erinn Banting, *Afghanistan the People* (New York: Crabtree Publishing Company, 2003).
34. Feisal Khan, "Why Borrow Trouble for yourself and Lend it to Neighbours? Understanding the Historical Roots of Pakistan Afghan Policy," *Asian Affairs: An American Review*, Vol. 37, Issue 04, October 2010.

35. For details about 1964 Constitution see, L. Dupree, *Afghanistan* (Princeton: Princeton University Press, 1973).
36. *Foreign Relations of the United States (FRUS),* Vol. 5, part 1, (US Government Printing Press, 1948).
37. Ganda Singh, "Ahmed Shah Durani: Father of Modern Afghanistan," (Bombay, Asia Publishing House, 1959).
38. Gen. Khalid Mahmud Arif, *Working with Zia: Pakistan's Power Politics, 1977-1988* (Karachi: Oxford University Press, 1995).
39. General Naseerullah Babur interview to A.H. Amin in March 2001, and published in a monthly *Defence Journal* (Rawalpindi: April 2001). See also Edward Girarde, *Afghanistan: the Soviet War* (Oxen: Routledge Publishers, 2011).
40. Hafez Malik, "Dilemmas of National Security and Cooperation," in *Dilemmas of National Security and Cooperation in India and Pakistan*, ed. Hafeez Malik, (London: Macmillan Press Ltd., 1993) Robert G. Wirsing, *Pakistan's Security Under Zia 1977-1988*, (New York: St. Martine's, 1991).
41. Harold G. Joseph, Political Stability on the North West Frontier of South Asia, (Washington, Foreign Service Institute, Department of State, 1951).
42. Hussain Haqqani, *Pakistan Between Mosque and Military* (Washington DC: Carnegie Endowment for International Peace, 2005).
43. I.D. Scott, Census of India 1941: North West Frontier Province (Delhi, Government of India), 1942, Vol. X.
44. I.H. Baqai, "Relations between Afghanistan and Pakistan," Pakistan Horizon, Vol. 1, No. 03, September 1948.
45. Ian Stephon, *Horned Moon* (London: Wrnest Benn, 1963).
46. Ian Talbot, *Pakistan: A modern History* (London: Hurst and company, 1998).

47. Iftikhar H. Malik, *The History of Pakistan* (London: Greenwood Press, 2008).
48. J.D. Cunningham, *A History of the Sikhs* (New Delhi, S. Chand, 1972).
49. J.W. Spain, "Pakistan North West Frontier," *Middle East Journal*, Vol. VIII, Winter 1954.
50. J.W. Spain, *The Pathan Borderland* (The Hauge, Mouton and Co., 1963).
51. Jagmohan Meher, "United States and Afghanistan: A Historical Perspective", in *South Asia Today,* ed. Goal Singh and Ramesh Chauhan (New Delhi: Anamika Publishers, 2005).
52. James W. Spain, "Pakistan's North West Frontier," *Middle East Journal,* Vol. 8, No. 1, (Washington DC: Winter 1954).
53. James. W Spaiin, "Political Problems of Borderland," in Ainslie T. Embree, ed., *Pakistan's Western Borderlands,* (New Delhi, 1977).
54. Jean-Luc Racine, "Pakistan in the Great Game", in *A History of Pakistan and its Origins,* ed. Christophe Jaffrelot (London: Anthem Press, 2002).
55. John C. Griffiths, *Afghanistan: Land of Conflict and Beauty* (London: Andre Deutsch, 2011).
56. Joseph Frankel, "*Contemporary International Theory and the Behaviour of States*," (London Oxford University Press, 1973).
57. K P Misra, *Afghanistan in Crisis* (New Delhi: Vikas Publishing House, 1981).
58. K Warikoo, *Afghanistan Challenges and Opportunities*, (New Delhi, Pentagon Press, 2007).
59. Kabul Mission diary, 12-16 November 1893.
60. F Progs., Nos. 71-158, N.A.I., December 1893, No. 154.
61. Kabul Times, 19 December 1973, the Hindustan Times, 30 July 1973 and The Times, 27 July 1973.

62. Kalim Bahadur, "Pakistan Foreign Policy Towards Afghanistan," *International Studies*, January 01, 1980.
63. Kalim Bahadur, "Pakistan's Policy Towards Afghanistan" in *Afghanistan in Crises,* ed. K P Mishra (New Delhi: Vikas Publishing House, 1981).
64. Kamal Matinuddin, *The Taliban Phenomenon: Afghanistan 1994-1997* (London: Oxford University Press, 2000).
65. Khan Ghazi Kabuli, the President of Pakhtoon Jirga-i-Hind, in a personal unstructured interview (New Delhi, 20 June 1981).
66. L.B. Polullada, "Pushtunistan: Afghan Domestic Politics and Relations with Pakistan," in A.T. Embreee, ed., *Pakistan Western Borderlands*, (New Delhi, Vishal, 1977).
67. L.F. Rushbrook Williams, *The State of Pakistan* (London, Faber and Faber 1966).
68. Ludwig W. Adamec, *Afghanistan 1990-1923: A Diplomatic History* (Berkeley, University of California Press, 1976).
69. M. Hussain Karkar, *Afghanistan: The Soviet invasion and the Afghan Response, 1979-1982* (Berkeley: California University Press, 1995).
70. M.A. Chaudhri, 'The Relations of Pakistan with Afghanistan,' *Pakistan Horizon*, Vol. viii, No. 04 December 1955.
71. M.A. Chaudhri, "The Relations of Pakistan with Afghanistan," *Pakistan Horizon*, Vol. Viii, No. 04, December 1955.
72. M.S. Agwani, "The Saur Revolution and After," *International Studies*, Vol. 19, No. 04, January 01, 1980.
73. Marvin G Weinbaum, *Pakistan and Afghanistan: Resistance and Reconstruction,* (San Francisco: Westview Press, 1994).

74. Marvin G Weinbaum, *Pakistan and Afghanistan: Resistance and Reconstruction* (San Francisco: Westview Press, 1994).

75. Mike Barry, *The Afghan Resistance from the Great Mongol till the Soviet Invasion* (Paris: Flammarion Publications, 1989).

76. Mohammad Ayub Khan, *Friends not Masters: A Political Autobiography*, (Lahore, Oxford University Press, 1967).

77. Mohammad Yahya. Akhter, "Electoral Politics and Corruption Under Civilian Rule in Post-1971 Pakistan," *South Asian Survey*, Vol. 11, Issue 01, January 03, 200.

78. Mohibullah Durani and Ashraf Khan, "Pakistan-Afghanistan Relations: Historical Mirror", *The Dialogue* Vol. 4, No. 1, (Peshawar: Jan-March 2009).

79. National Assembly Debates, Vol. V, No.03, 18 July 1974.

80. Neville Maxell, *India's China War*, (Bombay, Jaico Publishing House, 1950).

81. Official Records of the UN General Assembly Plenary Meeting, Ninety-Second Plenary Meeting, September 30, 1947, "Admission of Pakistan and Yemen to Membership in the United Nations," Document A/399.

82. Olof Caroe, *The Pathans, 550 B.C.-1957 A.D.* (London, Oxford University Press, 1965).

83. Pakistan Horizon, Vol. XXI, No.04, 1968, p. 379 and Pakistan Times, 24 December 1968.

84. Peshawar Confidential Diary, No. 19, dated 23 September 1893, For Dept. Sec., F. Progs., Nos 175-183, N.A.I., November 1893, No. 175 (Kabul Mission-1).

85. President Mohammad Daoud's speech at Lahore in *Foreign Affairs – Pakistan,* Islamabad: Ministry of Foreign Affairs, Vol. VI, Issue 3, March 1978.

86. Pyare Lal, *Mahatma Gandhi-The Last Phase* (Allahabad, Navajevan, 1956).
87. Rahaman Pazhwak, *Pakhtoonistan: The Khyber Pass as the Focus of the New State of Pakhtunistan* (London, n.p., n.d.).
88. Rahul Roy Chaudhury, "Pakistan", in *Afghanistan: To 2015 and Beyond,* ed. Toby Dodge and Nicholas Redman (Routledge: 2012).
89. Raiz Mohammad Khan, *Afghanistan and Pakistan: Conflict, Extremism, and Resistance to Modernity* (New Delhi: Oxford University Press, 2011).
90. Rasul Bakhsh Rais, "Afghanistan and Pakistan: Difficult Neighbours", *NBR Analysis,* Vol. 19, No. 5, (Washington DC: December 2008).
91. Rasul Bakhsh Rais, *Recovering the Frontier State: War, Ethnicity and State in Afghanistan* (Plymouth, UK: Lexington Books, 2008).
92. Rifaat Hussain, "Pakistan's Relations with Afghanistan: Continuity and Change", *www.docstoc.com/docs/24097140/pakistan-s-relations-with-afghanistan-continuity-and-change.*
93. Mujtaba Razvi, *The Frontiers of Pakistan: A Study of Frontier Problems in Pakistan's Foreign Policy* (Karachi: National Publishing House, 1971).
94. Rizwan Hussain, *Pakistan and the Emergence of Islamic Militancy in Afghanistan* (Hampshire: Ashgate Publishing Ltd., 2005).
95. Rizwan Hussain, *Pakistan and the Emergence of Islamic Militancy in Afghanistan,* 94.
96. Rob Johnson, *A Region in Turmoil: South Asian Conflicts Since 1947* (London: Reaktion Books, 2005).
97. S.M. Burke, *Pakistan's Foreign Policy* (London, Oxford University Press, 1973).
98. S.M. Qureshi, "The Frontier Dispute between Afghanistan and Pakistan," *Pacific Affairs*, Vol. XXXIX, Nos 1 and 2, Spring-Summer, 1966.

99. Sayed Yousuf Raza, "Pak Young Turks threaten Action," *The Tribune*, 26 January 1979.
100. Selig S. Harrison quoted in *Jihad Groups, Nuclear Pakistan and the New Great Game,* ed. M. Ahsan Ahrari (Carlisle, PA: Strategic Studies Institute, US Army War College, August 2001).
101. Selig S. Harrison, "Inside the Afghan Talks", *Foreign Policy,* no. 72, (Washington: Autumn 1988).
102. Hussain Haqqani, "Breaking Up is Not Hard to Do", *Foreign Affairs*, Vol. 92, No. 2, (New York: March-April 2013).
103. Selig S. Harrison, *In Afghanistan's Shadow: Balouch Nationalism and Soviet Temptation,* (New York: Carnegie Endowment for International Peace, 1981).
104. Shaista Wahab and Barry Youngerman, *A Brief History of Afghanistan* (New York: Infobase Publishing, 2007).
105. Shirin Tahir-Kheli "The Foreign Policy of New Pakistan," Orbis, Bol. XX, No. 03, Fall 1976.
106. Sir Percy Sykes, *Sir Mortimer Duran: A Biography* (London, Macmillan, 1926).
107. Sir William Barton, *India's North West Frontier* (London, Murray, 1939).
108. Stephen Tanner, *Afghanistan: A Military History from Alexander the Great to the Fall of Taliban* (USA: Da Capo Press, 2003).
109. Steve Coll, *Ghost Wars* (New York: Penguin Books, 2004).
110. Surendra Chopra, "Indo-Pakistan Relations: A Study of New Challenge and opportunities," in Surendra Chopra, ed., *Studies in India's Foreign Policy* (Amritsar, Gurunank Dev University, 1983).
111. Tehseena Usman, "Trust Deficit in Pak-Afghan Relations and its Implications: A Historical Perspective (1947-2001)," *Dialogue,* (1819-6462), 2013.

112. Telegram from the Department of State to the Embassy in Afghanistan, *FRUS*, 1961-63, Vol. XIX, South Asia.
113. The Afghans Nervous End Game, *The Economist* (US), April 25, 1992.
114. UN documents. A/PV. 1770, 29 September 1969, p. 04 and the Guardian, 7 June 1976.
115. Uzbekistan Area Handbook Series, *Afghanistan: A Country Study* (Baton Rouge: Claitor's Publishing Division, 2001).
116. W.K. Fraser Tytler, n.04, p.188. also cited by R.H.K., "The Durand Line," *Afghanistan News*, Vol. V, No. 62, October 1962.
117. W.K. Fraser Tytler, *Afghanistan: A study of Political Development in Central Asia* (London, Oxford University Press, 1950).
118. William Maley, *The Afghanistan Wars* (Hampshire: Palgrave Macmillan, 2002).
119. Z. Hilali, "The Soviet Penetration into Afghanistan and the Marxist Coup", *The Journal of Slavic Military Studies*, Vol. 18, no. 4 (London).
120. Ziba Moshaver, *Nuclear Weapons Proliferation in the Indian Subcontinent* (New York: St. Martin's Press, 1991).
121. Zubeida Hasan, 'The Foreign Policy of Afghanistan,' *Pakistan Horizon*, Vol. XVII, No. 01, 1964.

INDEX